Did Pocahontas Save Captain John Smith?

King Powhatan comāds C. Smith to be slayne, his daughter Pokahontas beggs his life his thankfullnes and how he subiected 39 of their kings. reade ŷ history.

Did Pocahontas Save Captain John Smith?

J. A. Leo Lemay

The University of Georgia Press   Athens and London

© 1992 by the University of Georgia Press
Athens, Georgia 30602
All rights reserved

Designed by Kathi L. Dailey
Set in Mergenthaler Janson Text by Tseng Information Systems, Inc.
Printed and bound by Thomson-Shore, Inc.
The paper in this book meets the guidelines for permanence and
durability of the Committee on Production Guidelines for Book
Longevity of the Council on Library Resources.

Printed in the United States of America

96 95 94 93 92   C   5 4 3 2 1

Library of Congress Cataloging in Publication Data

Lemay, J. A. Leo (Joseph A. Leo), 1935–
    Did Pocahontas save Captain John Smith? / J. A. Leo Lemay.
    p. cm.
    Includes bibliographical references and index.
    ISBN 0-8203-1461-7 (alk. paper)
    1. Smith, John, 1580–1631. 2. Pocahontas, d. 1617.
    3. Jamestown (Va.)—History. 4. Powhatan Indians—History.
    I. Title.
F229.S7L47 1992
973.2'1'092—dc20   92-791
                                                           CIP

British Library Cataloging in Publication Data available

Title page illustration: "King Powhatan commands C: Smith
to be slayne" (from the map of "Ould Virginia," in
John Smith, *True Travels*, 1630)

For Lorna and Wayne Craven

Contents

Acknowledgments

Darin Fields, my research assistant from 1989 to 1991, helped in every way throughout the preparation of this monograph. Susan Stabile, my research assistant during the 1991–92 academic year, read the finished manuscript and prepared the index. The Huntington Library, San Marino, California, generously granted permission to use the three illustrations. Celeste Walker of *The Adams Papers*, Massachusetts Historical Society, located Henry Adams's original manuscript of "Captain John Smith" for me, and Roger Stoddard of the Houghton Library, Harvard University, quickly supplied me with a photocopy. I am grateful to the librarians and staff of the Folger Shakespeare Library, the Library of Congress, and the University of Delaware Library for assistance while I worked on this monograph.

Prologue

Having feasted him [Smith] after their best barbarous manner they could, a long consultation was held, but the conclusion was, two great stones were brought before Powhatan: then as many as could layd hands on him, dragged him to them, and thereon laid his head, and being ready with their clubs, to beate out his braines, Pocahontas the Kings dearest daughter, when no intreaty could prevaile, got his head in her armes, and laid her owne upon his to save him from death: whereat the Emperour was contented he should live to make him hatchets, and her bells, beads, and copper. (Barbour, ed., *Complete Works* 2:150–51)

Did it really happen?

Did Pocahontas, on December 31, 1607, throw her head between Captain John Smith's and the tomahawks descending on his brains?

From 1860 to the present scholars have disagreed, but no one in the twentieth century has carefully examined the question.

Chronology

1579/80   January 9: John Smith baptized in Willoughby, England.

c. 1595–96   Pocahontas born.

1596–98   Smith served with English troops, perhaps under Lieutenant (later Captain) Joseph Duxbury, in the Netherlands.

1599–1600   Smith probably back in England.

1601–2   Smith joined the Imperial Army, assisted in a successful battle at Olumpagh (Lindava, Hungary) against the Turks, and was made captain of 250 cavalry. During a siege in the spring of 1602 he won the chance to duel in single combat against a Turkish champion. After conquering in the first duel, he fought and defeated two more champions in single combat. He was rewarded with a pension, the right to decorate his shield with three Turks' heads, and the title of English gentleman. Wounded in a later battle at Rottenton, he was left for dead on the field. Taken up by scavengers, he was sent to Istanbul, where he was sold as a slave.

Chronology

1603   In the fall Smith killed his owner near the Black Sea and made his way to Russia, whence he journeyed to eastern Europe.

1604/5   After various misadventures, Smith returned to England in the winter.

1606   December 19–20: The first Virginia Company colonists, including Smith, set sail.

1607   April 26: The original colonists arrived in Virginia.

    May 13: The colonists settled at Jamestown.

    c. December 12: Smith, exploring the upper Chickahominy, was captured by Opechancanough, Powhatan's younger brother.

    December 30: Smith taken before Powhatan.

    December 31: Concluding a ritual, Powhatan condemned Smith to death. Pocahontas pleaded for his life, and when the warriors were about to beat out his brains, she covered his head with hers. Powhatan then freed Smith, gave him "the Country of Capahowosick," and told him that Powhatan would "for ever esteeme him as his sonne Nantaquoud" (Barbour, ed., *Complete Works* 2:151).

1607/8   January 1: After a ceremony, Powhatan sent Smith back to Jamestown.

    February: "Now ever once in foure or five dayes, Pocahontas with her attendants, brought him so much provision, that saved many of their lives, that els for all this had starved with hunger" (2:152).

1608   May: Indians, even within Jamestown, began seizing guns, swords, and tools from the whites and shooting at them outside the fort. Smith took Indian captives and learned from Macanoe, a Paspahegh councillor, that the Indians "were directed onely by Powhatan to obtaine him our weapons, to cut our owne throats." After Smith gave the "prisoners what correction he thought fit," he "used them well for a day or two after, and then delivered them to Pocahontas, for whose sake onely he fayned to have saved their lives, and gave them liberty" (2:160).

August 13: Smith's *A True Relation* entered in the Stationers' Register. In a history of the colony's first year and a half in Virginia, Smith wrote an account of his captivity but did not mention Pocahontas's saving him. The entire narrative of his captivity, which consisted mainly of geographical and ethnological observations, was told in approximately 2,600 words.

September 10: Smith elected president of the Virginia Council.

October: Smith, with four whites and Namontack, went to Werowocomoco to prepare for Powhatan's coronation. Powhatan was sent for, but meanwhile "Pocahontas and her women entertained" Smith with "A Virginia Maske" (1:236; 2:183).

1608/9   January 12: Smith arrived at Werowocomoco to trade with Powhatan. About ten days later, when Smith was preparing to leave, Pocahontas came to warn him that Powhatan intended to ambush him and his men later that night.

late January: Richard Wiffin rushed to Werowocomoco with the news that Matthew Scrivener, Captain Richard Waldo, Anthony Gosnold, and others had drowned in the James River. Smith, however, had already left for Pamunkey. Powhatan ordered Wiffin killed, but Pocahontas hid him and told Powhatan that Wiffin had gone off in a different direction (2:203–4).

1609   early September: Sailing down the James River, Smith was incapacitated, his genitals probably mutilated, by a gunpowder explosion, which caused a severe burn. He shipped for England by early October.

November 30: Before this date, Smith arrived in England.

c. December: John Ratcliffe (alias Sickelmore) attempted to trade with Powhatan, but he neglected to keep guard and was killed with about thirty men; "only Jeffrey Shortridge escaped, and Pokahontas the Kings daughter saved a boy called Henry Spelman" (2:232).

1612   Smith's *Map of Virginia* published. This
        geographical and ethnological account
        accompanied the Virginia map he had published
        slightly earlier. He did not mention his
        captivity, but in describing one of the three
        methods Indians were executed, he alluded to
        the way he was about to be killed when
        Pocahontas saved him. *The Proceedings*,
        technically part 2 of *A Map of Virginia*, tells the
        history of Virginia from 1606 to 1612,
        describing in about eighty words the story of
        Smith's captivity, with no mention of
        Pocahontas.

1613   April: Captain Samuel Argall captured
        Pocahontas and arrived at Jamestown with her
        on April 13.

1614   c. April 5: The Reverend Richard Bucke
        married Pocahontas and John Rolfe at
        Jamestown.

        March–August: Smith explored the New
        England coast.

1615   Thomas Rolfe, son of Pocahontas and
        John, born.

1616   c. April 21: Rolfe family sailed for England with
        Thomas Dale and Captain Samuel Argall.

        June 3: Smith's *Description of New England*
        entered in the Stationers' Register. The same
        day, Dale, Rolfe, Pocahontas, Uttamatomakkin
        and his wife, Matachauna (Pocahontas's sister),

two Indian maidens, and several other Indians arrived at Plymouth, England.

June 18: Smith's *Description of New England* published. Shortly thereafter Smith delivered it to Prince Charles (later Charles I), who substituted English for some Indian place-names. Probably at the same time, Smith presented a letter to Queen Anne telling of Pocahontas's various services to the whites in Virginia, including a detail of her saving him: "At the minute of my execution, she hazarded the beating out of her owne braines to save mine" (2:259). The letter, however, is only known from its publication in Smith's *Generall Historie* (1624).

1616/17   January 6: Pocahontas and Uttamatomakkin attended Ben Jonson's court masque, *The Vision of Delight*. King James I and Queen Anne were also present.

March: Pocahontas, ill, sailed for Virginia but died before clearing England. On March 21 she was buried at Gravesend. The infant Thomas Rolfe remained in England.

1618   April: Powhatan died.

1621   May 2: Smith petitioned the Virginia Company for reward but received nothing (Kingsbury 1:460).

1622   early spring: John Rolfe evidently died of illness.

March 22: Opechancanough led the Virginia massacre.

October: In an expanded edition of *New Englands Trials* (first published in 1620), Smith advertised himself as an Indian expert who had bested Opechancanough, leader of the late massacre, though he conceded that the Indians had earlier captured him, "yet God made Pocahontas the King's daughter the means to deliver me" (Barbour, ed., *Complete Works* 1:432). Thus he mentioned for the first time in print that Pocahontas had saved him.

1623   A commission for an investigation of the Virginia Company was drawn up by April 22 and issued May 8. Sir William Jones headed the commission. Smith testified in May or early June, mentioning that he had been captured by the Indians and that Pocahontas had been "the means to returne me safe to James towne" (2:323). His testimony is known only from its publication in *The Generall Historie* (1624).

summer or fall: Smith published a prospectus of *The Generall Historie*, mentioning the Pocahontas incident.

1624   July 12: Smith's *Generall Historie* entered into the Stationers' Register. Book 2 slightly revised and expanded the geographical and ethnological materials in *A Map of Virginia*. Book 3 revised and expanded the colony's history as told in *The Proceedings*. Whereas the story of Smith's

captivity in *A True Relation*, including
geographical and ethnological information,
took approximately 2,600 words and the version
in *The Proceedings*, omitting the geographical
and ethnological information that appeared in *A
Map*, took approximately 80 words, the version
in Book 3 expanded the 80 words to
approximately 1,900 words.

1629   August 29: *The True Travels* was entered into the
        Stationers' Register. Published in 1630, it
        mentioned that Powhatan "commanded him to
        be slaine" and that "*Pocahontas* saved his life"
        (3:237).

1630   June 21: Smith died and was buried at St.
        Sepulchre's Church, London.

1644   April: Opechancanough, after leading another
        Indian uprising, was killed.

Did Pocahontas Save Captain John Smith?

Introduction

In the age of nationalism that followed the American Revolution and the War of 1812, historians and writers celebrated and mythologized the Founding Fathers, such as George Washington, Thomas Jefferson, John Adams, and Benjamin Franklin, as well as the early American explorers and settlers, including Virginia Dare and the Lost Colony, Captain John Smith and Jamestown, William Bradford and Plymouth Colony, and John Winthrop and the Massachusetts Bay Colony. Just as George Washington became the most celebrated Founding Father, so Captain John Smith became the best-known early American explorer and settler. His name and the story of his being saved by Pocahontas appeared in all the standard American histories, including those by William Robertson (1801), Justice John Marshall (1804), James Grahame (1827), and George Bancroft (1834), as well as in the numerous histories written for schools and in the biographies of Americans compiled for children.[1]

In the early nineteenth century, a special genre, the Indian play, became popular onstage, and most Indian plays mentioned Smith and Pocahontas. Several featured them: J. N. Barker's *The Indian Princess* (1808), George Washington Parke

1

Custis's *Pocahontas* (1830), Robert Dale Owen's *Pocahontas* (1837), and Charlotte Barnes's *The Forest Princess* (1844). After a half century of popularity, the genre in general and the Smith-Pocahontas story in particular were wonderfully burlesqued by John Brougham's *Po-ca-hon-tas* (1855). The burlesque, however, was not meant to attack either Smith or Pocahontas. It parodied the Indian dramas. During the same period novelists and poets also devoted volumes or major parts of books to Smith and Pocahontas: John Davis in 1805, St. Leger Carter in 1821, John Pendleton Kennedy in 1832, Mrs. M. M. Webster in 1840, Lydia Huntley Sigourney in 1841, Seba Smith in 1841, William Gilmore Simms in 1845, and William Makepeace Thackeray in 1857.

By the mid–nineteenth century Captain John Smith was as well known to Americans as any figure from American history, save, possibly, George Washington. A few historians and writers cast some doubt upon the "romantick" nature of Smith's numerous adventures, but these doubts were rare and minor in a chorus of praise. Because of his extraordinary feats, assertive personality, and yeoman background and because his adventures occurred in faraway and exotic places, a few skeptics from the seventeenth to the mid–nineteenth century said that Captain John Smith might be a fraud. The first scholar to question a specific detail and to give reasons for not believing Smith was the Boston historian and businessman Charles Deane in notes to his 1860 edition of Edward Maria Wingfield's "A Discourse of Virginia." Deane argued that Pocahontas did not save Smith. Henry Adams followed Deane with a full-scale attack in 1867. Since 1860 scholars have disagreed, but the last person to devote a separate essay to details of the argument was Henry Adams, in the 1891 revision of his 1867 article. From 1891 to the present numerous persons have taken sides on the question. The prevailing judgment, cited in many recent histories of the United States and in anthologies of American literature, is that we will never know the truth of the Smith-Pocahontas episode. But no full analysis of the "Great Debate," as Bradford Smith called the question, has been attempted since 1891.

I recently read all the Smith scholarship and was surprised that modern scholars completely disagreed about whether or not Pocahontas saved Captain John Smith. Some believed she did, some believed the supposed fact was romantic nonsense, and the nonspecialists seemed to think it impossible to know the truth. The longest twentieth-century discussion appeared in Bradford Smith's biography, *Captain John Smith* (1953), but Smith did not refute Henry Adams's arguments from 1867, 1871, and 1891, did not cite William Wirt Henry's 1875 valuable rebuttal of Adams, made a few dubious arguments, and failed to convince a number of reviewers and subsequent scholars.

After rereading Captain John Smith with admiration for his ability, accomplishments, and character, I believed he must have been telling the truth. But could I prove it? At first I was uncertain. I think that if I had found that the facts proved Smith a liar, I would have labeled him one. But as I analyzed the evidence, I became convinced beyond a reasonable doubt that he told the truth. Pocahontas saved him. Why, then, did he not mention it in his three early Virginia tracts? The first two sections of chapter 2 attempt to answer that question.

It is surprising that William Wirt Henry's excellent 1875 refutation of Henry Adams's essay is not better known. Considerations having little to do with the quality of Adams's or Henry's arguments are probably responsible. The *North American Review*, where Adams published his attack, was the best known and most respected magazine of its day in America.

Potter's American Monthly, where William Wirt Henry published his refutation, was a popular but minor magazine. Another major consideration concerning Smith's reputation was the appearance of Lewis L. Kropf's 1890 attack on Smith's Balkan adventures, supposedly proving that Smith lied about them. Kropf reinforced the opinion that Smith was a braggart and a liar.

Further, Adams's attack on Smith began as part of his anti-Southern campaign. Adams wrote it in 1862 as war propaganda. In a letter to John Gorham Palfrey, Adams called it a kind of "flank attack" upon the South and said that the "Virginia aristocracy . . . will be utterly gravelled by it." Adams knew well that John Randolph of Roanoke (1773–1833), a major opponent of both his great-grandfather John Adams and his grandfather John Quincy Adams, was proud of his descent from Pocahontas. Adams said in the same March 20, 1862, letter to Palfrey: "I can imagine to myself the shade of John Randolf turn green at that quaint picture which Strachey gives of Pocahontas 'clothed in virgin purity' and 'wanton' at that, turning somersets with all the little ragamuffins and 'decayed serving-men's' sons of Jamestowne."[2] Henry Adams directly maligned the Virginian in his 1882 biography *John Randolph*, but he meant the article on Captain John Smith to censure Randolph and all the numerous Virginia descendants of Pocahontas in addition to tarnishing the reputation of the South's greatest early hero, Captain John Smith. Adams labeled the monumental Southern superstar a pitiful liar. He would prove that the haughty Randolph and the proud Virginians based their traditions upon a fraud. So long as post–Civil War animosities against the South remained and so long as South-baiting persisted, attacks on Smith often reflected anti-Southern feelings.

A final consideration concerns the modern reputations of

Henry Adams and William Wirt Henry. During the twentieth century Henry Adams has increasingly come to be recognized as a major American writer, achieving the distinction of a separate chapter in Robert E. Spiller's *Literary History of the United States* (1948). He has since been the subject of a number of appreciative books and essays. He may be more famous now than he was while alive. On the other hand, William Wirt Henry, though achieving the eminence of president of the American Historical Association for 1890–91, has been comparatively forgotten.

Since I have been able to add to the arguments of Henry Adams and William Wirt Henry, I should say that it is infinitely easier to be an accurate literary historian and scholar in the twentieth century than it was in the nineteenth. I photocopied relevant pages of the different editions of Samuel Purchas's works from conveniently available microfilms in the University of Delaware Library and marked up my own copy of Captain John Smith's *Complete Works*, which exists in an excellent annotated and indexed edition. Henry Adams and, especially, William Wirt Henry researched and wrote under less favorable conditions. Adams wrote in the British Museum, using Smith's original publications but without the excellent notes of Philip L. Barbour's 1986 edition. William Wirt Henry wrote in Virginia, with access to only a few major texts of Smith and his contemporaries. I would like to think that if Henry Adams had been able to photocopy the relevant pages of the different editions of Samuel Purchas's works, he might not have confused them and that if he had been able to mark up his own copy of *The Complete Works of Captain John Smith*, he might not have overlooked pertinent evidence and misrepresented other details. But Adams wrote his essay in 1862 and early 1863, not only without these late twentieth-century conveniences but also in the midst of the most damaging war that America has ever fought, the Civil War. He wrote as a partisan. Though his opponent William Wirt Henry had the better arguments and won (in my opinion) the historical battle, Henry's refutation has been ignored or forgotten. Henry Adams won the war.

In chapter 1, I survey the history of the dispute and set it within the context of the changing general reputation of Captain John Smith. Chapter 2 examines the appearance (and absence) of the Pocahontas episode in Smith's writings. I pay more attention to the pertinent circumstances of each mention of the Pocahontas episode in Smith's works than has any previous writer. Chapter 3 gathers together and analyzes the other evidence, pro and con, that bears upon the debate. A brief conclusion summarizes my findings, and an afterword catalogs Henry Adams's errors.

ONE

History of the Dispute

Henry Adams (1838–1918) wrote in 1867 that "every historian should hereafter take one side or the other in regard to this question" about Pocahontas and Captain John Smith. Adams, the great-grandson of the Massachusetts Revolutionary patriot John Adams, maintained in the *North American Review*'s lead article for January 1867 that Smith lied and that Pocahontas did not save him. Eight years after Adams attacked Smith, William Wirt Henry (1831–1900), grandson of the Virginia Revolutionary patriot Patrick Henry, refuted Adams.[1] Adams's attack has been reprinted in revised versions numerous times and is well known and often cited.[2] Henry's refutation in *Potter's American Monthly* for 1875, however, was only once reprinted (with a mishmash of additional material) and is comparatively unknown.[3] Years later, reflecting upon his bold entrance into colonial historiography in *The Education of Henry Adams*, Adams explained that John Gorham Palfrey suggested in the spring of 1861 that an attack on Smith "would attract as much attention, and probably break as much glass as any other stone that could be thrown by a beginner."[4]

Palfrey, a New England historian and a close friend of

Pocahontas (from John Smith, *Generall Historie*, 1624)

Adams's father, said he was "haunted by incredulity" regarding various episodes in Smith's life.[5] Palfrey knew and was influenced by Charles Deane's 1860 questioning of the episode's truth.[6] Palfrey's doubt of Smith and encouragement of Adams, together with Charles Deane's writings, have ever since poisoned the well. When Jarvis M. Morse reviewed the Smith historiography in 1935, he dismissed the Pocahontas story as a "petty detail" and as "unimportant."[7] Morse considered Smith's contributions to the exploration and settlement of Virginia and New England so many and so important that the truth of the Smith-Pocahontas episode was, in comparison, insignificant. Though Morse's point of view has some validity, I also think that it is important to know whether Smith lied — and lied and lied — about Pocahontas. Was he a vainglorious liar, capitalizing upon the momentary fame of Pocahontas, as various historians have claimed since 1860? Or was he truthful?

Morse did not cite and evidently did not know William Wirt Henry's focused refutation of Adams; instead he cited Henry's mishmash of arguments against Adams, the Reverend Edward D. Neill, and others, as delivered in a lecture before the Virginia Historical Society in 1882.[8] Despite not using Henry's better essay and not reviewing the Pocahontas episode in detail, Morse concluded: "Whatever mental reservations one may have as to the probability of the incident, by no sound application of the laws of historical testimony can it be disproved, save by the appearance of contrary evidence yet undiscovered."[9] It cannot be disproved, but why approach the question from the negative? Why take the defensive? Can one prove that Pocahontas did save Captain John Smith?[10]

Contemporary writers and literary scholars still often maintain that Smith lied about the Pocahontas episode. Elizabeth Stevenson, editor of *A Henry Adams Reader* (1958), commented that the story of Pocahontas's saving Captain John Smith is "one of the old American myths." The Captain John Smith "Secret Journal" portions of John Barth's wonderful novel *The Sot-Weed Factor* (1960) partially depend for their effect upon Smith's supposed reputation for lying and vainglory. Philip Young felt obliged to begin his 1962 essay on the archetypal implications of the Pocahontas story with the words "Of course it may not have happened at all." Henry B. Rule believed that Adams was correct: in 1962 Rule said that one of Adams's purposes was to satirize "the romantic historian [George Bancroft] who was more interested in a pretty story than in checking the facts," and he referred to the "vulgar reality presented by documentary evidence" regarding Pocahontas. Ernest Samuels's 1974 note on Henry Adams's statement in *The Education* assumes that Smith lied: "Adams's article disproving Smith's account of his rescue by Pocahontas outraged many patriotic Virginians."[11]

Despite Bradford Smith's *Captain John Smith: His Life and Legend* (1953), Philip L. Barbour's splendid biography *The Three Worlds of Captain John Smith* (1964) and his thoroughly annotated three-volume edition of *The Complete Works of Captain John Smith* (1986), some fine historians remain unconvinced. They believe that Henry Adams revealed the truth. Though Jarvis Morse, reviewing Bradford Smith in the *Mississippi Valley Historical Review* in 1954, found evidence for changing his mind and now thought that Bradford Smith's biography "should put an end to that ruckus" (the charge that Smith lied about either his Balkan adventures or the Pocahontas episode), not all reviewers were satisfied. Jane Whitehill, writing in the *William and Mary Quarterly*, also in 1954, found that "many doubts are still conceivable" and reiterated the point that "not until Pocahontas was dead (but still a celebrity) did Smith first print" the Pocahontas story.[12]

Reviewing Barbour's *Three Worlds* in the *Journal of American History*, Richard Beale Davis pointed out that Smith's version of the Pocahontas episode was now generally accepted by twentieth-century scholars simply because Smith was now considered "remarkably accurate in his account" of his eastern European career. But Michael G. Hall, in the *American Historical Review*, criticized Barbour for accepting Smith. Hall said Barbour's hypotheses were reasonable for some simple situations, "but to explain the 'facts' about Smith's rescue by Pocahontas is a more difficult matter altogether. Too often Barbour's case seems to me unproved." Barbour himself sometimes seemed uncertain of what happened. Though he argued for the truth of the Pocahontas episode in *The Three Worlds of Captain John Smith* and though he told the story without questioning it in *Pocahontas and Her World* (1970), he expressed some doubt in his article "Pocahontas" for the biographical dictionary *Notable American Women, 1607–1950* (1971). There, he quoted Smith's letter to Queen Anne in 1616 and then commented, "Later, in 1624, the account was vividly expanded, with what regard for the truth is not known."[13]

Some reviewers of Philip L. Barbour's edition of *The Complete Works of Captain John Smith* still saw no reason to believe Smith. Thomas P. Slaughter, writing in *Reviews in American History*, said that Smith "baldly transformed the famous story of his brief captivity by Indians from a tale of tribal nobility to an adventure-romance in which Smith was delivered from imminent decapitation [*sic*] through the direct intercession of Pocahontas. After years of recounting his experiences in founding Virginia, Smith suddenly included the Indian maiden in the story, *after* she had become an English celebrity of sorts, and *after* her death and the demise of all others who might prove the lie to his revised version." Slaughter concluded, "Adams was on solid ground with his debunking of Smith, and he was justified in exposing 'falsehoods of an effrontery seldom equalled in modern times.' "[14]

Bernard W. Sheehan, reviewing Barbour's edition in the *American Historical Review*, wrote: "On the Pocahontas story the revisionist argument does ring a bit hollow. We have long been told that Smith omitted Pocahontas's role . . . from *A True Relation* because he wished to stay in the company's good graces by avoiding reference to Indian hostility. But the work contains other and more telling evidence of native hostility, and Smith did not intend any of it for publication, which leaves one wondering whether in his later, more formal, *Generall Historie* he did not succumb to the temptation to embroider a good story. Fortunately, the value of Smith as a source does not hinge on his relationship with Pocahontas."[15]

Reflecting the opposite point of view, James Axtell, writing in the London *Times Literary Supplement*, flatly stated that Henry Adams and other late nineteenth-century doubters "were wrong." Axtell said that "since the 1950s, when qualified scholars began to scrutinize his pre-American career, nothing has been found to discredit the essential truth of anything he wrote." Axtell added, "The same is true for the remainder of his experiences." Eugene R. Sheridan thought that "Barbour's edition marks what may well be the final step in Smith's vindication against the criticisms of a long line of detractors." Alden Vaughan has wavered back and forth on the issue. In his 1975 monograph *American Genesis: Captain John Smith and the Founding of Virginia*, he seemed to think the truth impossible to know: "The truth lies buried with the captain and his

Indian captors." Reviewing Barbour's *Complete Works* in the *New York Times Book Review*, he guardedly thought that Smith told the truth: "By the mid-1960s, a clear scholarly consensus supported Smith's truthfulness and there was a new appreciation of his role in fostering England's American empire." [16] But in 1988 he again had doubts. Writing about a 1631 satire on Smith, Vaughan said that the skepticism of Henry Adams "may reflect more accurately the opinion of Smith's own era than do Bradford Smith's and Philip Barbour's testimonials." [17] Actually, in almost all the twentieth-century reexaminations of Smith's veracity, little critical attention has been paid to the story that first called his truthfulness into question—his account of being saved by Pocahontas.

Instead, Smith's reputation has been entirely and inextricably bound up with his eastern European adventures of 1601–3. A Hungarian scholar, Lewis L. Kropf, published a series of articles on Smith in 1890, citing Hungarian sources that most American and English historians could not read, arguing that Smith lied about his adventures, and concluding that he had probably never been to eastern Europe. For most historians of the next sixty-three years, Kropf completely discredited Smith. J. Franklin Jameson labeled the Pocahontas story a lie in 1891. Yale's Herbert L. Osgood, in his masterful 1904–7 study *The American Colonies in the Seventeenth Century*, warily avoided mentioning it.[18] Harvard's Albert Bushnell Hart included Smith in 1915 in a series of "American Historical Liars." Harvard's Samuel Eliot Morison wrote in 1930 that "very little" of the Balkan adventures "could possibly have happened" and called Smith's patent of arms from Prince Sigismund "a palpable forgery." [19] That same year, Lawrence C. Wroth was more circumspect but nevertheless could do little to free Smith's reputation from the nadir to which it had fallen:

"Kropf's argument is not unassailable in many particulars, but its general tendency may be refuted only by one as thoroughly at home as its author in the geography and the history of the Balkans."[20] Believing that Smith's eastern European adventures had been proven to be fabrications, almost all historians assumed that he also lied about his American experiences. Two major late nineteenth-century Virginia historians, Edward D. Neill and Alexander Brown, also contributed to Smith's unsavory reputation. Following Charles Deane and Henry Adams, they repeatedly maligned Smith and created their own interpretation of early Virginia history, in which Smith was labeled time and again a liar.[21] Susan M. Kingsbury's publication, however, between 1906 and 1935 of *The Records of the Virginia Company* provided a mass of contemporary evidence validating Smith's statements and opinions concerning early Virginia. Wesley Frank Craven discovered that the Virginia Company records made Smith's opinions not only perceptive but also prescient.[22] Thus in his historiographic essay Jarvis Morse could celebrate Smith's contributions to colonization in America, especially Virginia. Despite the increasing recognition that Smith made enormous contributions to the exploration and settlement of America, almost everyone still thought Smith probably made up the Pocahontas episode and his exotic adventures in eastern Europe. The only major academic historian between 1890 and 1950 to suggest that the Pocahontas story "can be shown to be true in all probability" was Yale's Charles M. Andrews. Alas, Andrews did not attempt to prove it.[23]

In 1953, sixty-three years after Kropf discredited Smith, Laura Polanyi Striker published "Captain John Smith's Hungary and Transylvania" as an appendix to Bradford Smith's biography, thoroughly refuting Kropf. Kropf overlooked, misread, and ignored evidence from the very sources he cited. Striker concluded that Smith's critics, especially Kropf, merited the words Smith "had once quoted out of Hakluyt: 'Oh incredulitie the wit of fooles, that slovingly doe spit at all things faire, a sluggards Cradle, a Cowards Castle, how easie it is to be an Infidell.' "[24] As Smith's account of warfare in the Balkans, contrary to Kropf's superficial and biased reporting, has been found to correspond with the actual history of the area in 1601–3, his general reputation has been rehabilitated without any serious reexamination of the Pocahontas episode. Even in an essay entitled "The Rehabilitation of Captain John Smith," Laura Polanyi Striker and Bradford Smith never mentioned Pocahontas or Smith's captivity. They assumed their proof that Captain John Smith was actually a good primary source for the history of eastern Europe in 1601–3 also certified that he told the truth about his Virginia adventures. As we have seen, however, that reasoning failed to convince a number of subsequent literary scholars and historians.

Henry Adams's 1867 essay attacking Smith in the *North American Review* ostensibly reviewed two editions by Charles Deane: Edward Maria Wingfield's "A Discourse of Virginia" (1860) and John Smith's *A True Relation of Virginia* (1866).[25] In his scholarly notes to Wingfield, Deane had pointed out that Smith did not mention the Pocahontas episode in his first Virginia account, the *True Relation* of 1608, or in the next two pamphlets he wrote, *A Map of Virginia* and *The Proceedings* of 1612.[26] Deane said that Smith only introduced the story after Pocahontas "had become somewhat famous in the annals of Virginia." He suggested that Smith changed the story of his captivity in order to "puff" himself. Deane remarked that the only evidence for the Smith-Pocahontas episode came from Smith. And Deane contended that if the story were true, Wingfield or some other person present in Virginia who left records of the time would have mentioned it.[27]

Urged on by his family friend John Gorham Palfrey, Henry Adams searched the British Museum for manuscript or printed evidence that would impugn Smith. He failed to find any evidence but instead reported that the known writings by Smith tended to convince him that Smith was telling the truth. He wrote Palfrey on October 23, 1861, that "on the whole I give it up, but would like to know if you think a case is still possible."[28] Palfrey's and Charles Deane's replies convinced Adams that he should go on with the project of denigrating Smith.[29] Adams persevered because the attack on Smith "is in some sort a flank, or rather a rear attack, on the Virginia aristocracy, who will be utterly gravelled by it if it is successful." Adams revealed later, on March 20, 1862, that what was most important to him in the attack was really the aspersions that he might be able to cast on Pocahontas, because she was the ancestor of a number of prominent Virginians, including John Randolph of Roanoke, a political opponent of his great-grandfather John Adams and grandfather John Quincy Adams. "I can imagine to myself the shade of John Randolf turn green at that quaint picture which Strachey gives of Pocahontas 'clothed in virgin purity' and 'wanton' at that, turning somersets with all the little ragamuffins and 'decayed serving men's' sons of Jamestowne.'"[30] By May 29, 1863, Adams had finished the essay and sent it to Palfrey. When Deane's edition of Smith's *A True Relation* appeared in 1866, Adams revised the essay and at Palfrey's suggestion sent it to the *North American Review*.[31]

Deane's scholarly editions drew comparatively little publicity. One amateur Virginia historian and descendant of Pocahontas, Wyndham Robertson, replied to Deane's edition of Wingfield in the year it appeared, 1860, but his arguments, though anticipating William Wirt Henry's in some details, were not as thorough as Henry's.³² "Smith's Rescue by Pocahontas," an anonymous review of Deane's edition, appeared in the *Southern Literary Messenger* in the November–December issue of 1862.³³ Deane chafed under the criticisms by this anonymous author and sent Henry Adams a copy of the review in 1867—long after Adams wrote his essay and some months after its publication. Adams replied to Deane that if he had seen the *Messenger* piece beforehand, "I should not have changed a line in my own, though I might perhaps have added a paragraph."³⁴ As we will see, Adams's later revisions take account of this reply to Deane and subsequent replies to Deane and Adams.

Although Robertson's 1860 article was reprinted in the *Historical Magazine* and was certainly read by Deane, it made no impression on him. Deane repeated and amplified his earlier criticisms when he edited Smith's *A True Relation* in 1866. Adams's attack appeared as the lead article in the *North American Review* for January 1867 and created, as Adams's biographer says, "its little sensation."³⁵ It was promptly noticed in a dozen periodicals and celebrated in the *Pall Mall Gazette* and *The Nation* as a splendid example of revisionist history.³⁶ Adams, however, did not mention Robertson. Likewise, though he attempted to answer the *Messenger* reviewer's criticisms of Deane in his 1871 revision of "Captain John Smith" in *Chapters of Erie, and Other Essays*, he did not mention the criticism. William Wirt Henry's 1875 examination of Adams's arguments might have had an effect on Adams except for the attacks on Smith by the Virginia authorities Edward D. Neill and Alexander Brown and especially the 1890 attack by the Hungarian historian Lewis L. Kropf. In the midst of this explosion of anti-Smith invective, Adams probably believed that he had led the way in unmasking Smith as a liar. So he again revised the essay for a selection of his best historical essays in 1891. Though he contended with William Wirt Henry's criticisms, he did not mention Henry, even though he had corresponded with him in 1877.[37] As I will show below, ordinary readers of Adams's essay—and even such careful scholars as Jarvis Morse—have not realized that Adams thoroughly revised his essay twice stylistically and factually, trying to cope with the arguments of the *Messenger* reviewer and William Wirt Henry. To the casual investigator, it might well still appear that Henry Adams had the best and the last words on the subject.

TWO

The Pocahontas Episode in Smith's Writings

In this chapter I will discuss the eight (or possibly nine) times that the Pocahontas episode appears in Smith's writings. Since Smith's critics have consistently claimed that Pocahontas did not save Smith because the event is not in his 1608 and 1612 writings, I will also discuss the possible reasons for its absence there.

A True Relation, 1608

Charles Deane and Henry Adams argued that if Pocahontas had really saved Captain John Smith, he would have told the story in his personal narrative of early Virginia, *A True Relation*.[1] Several points about this should be made. *A True Relation* was the first published tract about the new colony. For reasons concerning public relations, the Virginia Company officials wanted the Indians to seem friendly. The Virginia Company editor, John Healey, admitted that he cut parts of Smith's report (1:24).[2] Reviewing Deane in 1860, Wyndham Robertson noted that Smith may have included the Pocahontas episode and that it may have been cut by the editor. The anonymous

Captain John Smith (from Smith's map of
New England, 1616)

1862 reviewer of Deane's edition of Wingfield's "Discourse" specifically argued that the editor cut the text of *A True Relation* at precisely the point where the Pocahontas episode should have been related and even theorized that the editor interpolated some of Smith's supposed text. William Wirt Henry (who may not have known either Robertson's review or the anonymous 1862 reply) in 1875 repeated the argument that *A True Relation* was evidently cut at the place where the Pocahontas episode should have been reported. Henry added that Smith (or his editor) deliberately downplayed the Indians' hostility in the tract.[3]

Nevertheless, as Frances Mossiker and others have pointed out, the killings of George Cassen, Thomas Emry, and John Robinson are all present in the 1608 account, as well as the story of several Indian attacks upon Jamestown.[4] Altogether, *A True Relation* contains considerable evidence of Indian hostility. Why, then, should the Pocahontas episode have been cut and these other evidences of antipathy left?

I find the argument that the editor cut out the Pocahontas episode to be weak. Throughout Smith's early writings, his syntax was often jumbled, he frequently hurried over the sequence of events, and he sometimes omitted necessary connections. These faults are more frequent in *A True Relation* than in his other writings. After all, he composed *A True Relation* as a letter to a friend. It was probably written quickly without revision or rewriting. There is no proof that the text was cut at the point where the Pocahontas episode could have been related. Furthermore, Smith specifically said that when he first met Powhatan, the chief "kindly welcomed me with good wordes, and great Platters of sundrie Victuals, assuring mee his friendship, and my libertie within foure dayes" (1:53). (The anonymous 1862 reviewer suggested that those words were interpolated by John Healey, but I reject the possibility as unfounded.) *A True Relation* concluded the passage on Smith's captivity with these words: "Thus having with all the kindnes hee could devise, sought to content me: he sent me home" (1:57). Charles Deane charged that *A True Relation* simply does not appear to be consistent with Smith's later story of being condemned to death and saved by Pocahontas.[5] I agree. Deane's point is excellent.

Deane later added another argument. In 1885 he published a brief piece on the history of the dispute, "Pocahontus and Captain Smith: A Reminiscence," in which he pointed out that Smith's notice of Pocahontas near the end of *A True Relation* constituted a full introduction and appreciation of her. Deane observed: "If there had been an elaborate story of Smith's rescue by Pocahontas while a prisoner with Powhatan, in the earlier part of the book, all this introduction and personal description of the young child near its close would have been as unnecessary as it would have been unnatural to the most unpracticed writer."[6] Deane scored again. I believe that Charles Deane all but proved that Smith did not include the Pocahontas episode in *A True Relation*.

A True Relation, however, does not begin to tell everything that happened to Smith during his first year in Virginia. It does not even describe all the life-threatening situations that occurred during his captivity. It is not an internally consistent fictional work, but a report of Smith's ever-changing impressions of reality. Deane and Adams emphasized Powhatan's friendly statements. If one focuses on the facts of the killing of George Cassen (by torture), John Robinson, and Thomas Emry and the attempted killing of Smith by the enraged Indian father, then another view of Smith's captivity might well emerge.

The Pocahontas Episode in Smith's Writings

Charles Deane wrote that in *A True Relation* Smith does not seem to have "considered his life at all in danger while he was a guest or prisoner of Powhatan."[7] Adams, though discounting one exception and noting another, echoed Deane:

> There is not a trace of his having felt any immediate fear for his life, except from a savage whose son he killed and from whom Opechankanough protected him. There does indeed occur one line to the effect that they fed him so fat as to make him much doubt they meant to sacrifice him [*CW* 1:59]; and this paragraph furnishes the most striking evidence of the kindness of the Indians, and of the fact that he believed himself to have been mistaken in having entertained the suspicion. Yet in 1624 we learn that all this long time of his imprisonment he was still expecting every hour to be put to one death or another.[8]

The *Southern Literary Messenger*'s reviewer replied to Deane but vitiated his point by citing *The Generall Historie* for proof rather than *A True Relation*.[9]

It appears only commonsensical to me that Smith could not help but think that the Indians might kill him at any time. He mentioned in *A Map of Virginia* that one method the Indians used to execute people was to throw them into a pit filled with flaming charcoal. William Strachey noted that Smith, while a captive, was brought "for some purpose" to see such an execution.[10] Smith commented in *A Map* that Powhatan thought the fresh scalps of the Payankatank Indians would frighten the whites who saw them (*CW* 1:175). Clearly Powhatan used his own version of psychological warfare. During his captivity, Smith had good reason to be frightened. Smith made no mention of his feelings upon seeing a victim thrown into a pit filled with flaming charcoal. Perhaps it didn't affect him, but personally, in Smith's position I would have been terrified. Further, Deane and Adams both overlooked or ignored Smith's 1608 statement that "at each place I expected when they would execute me" (1:47). Regarding Smith's anxiety, Deane and Adams are simply wrong.

Inconsistencies exist in *A True Relation*. I believe they existed during Smith's captivity. In *The Generall Historie*, Smith wrote that after Pocahontas saved him, Powhatan said Smith "should live to make him hatchets, and her bells, beads, and copper." Immediately after that sentence, Smith wrote that one day later, Powhatan, after performing a ritual "behind a mat" in a "great house in the woods," came with two hundred Indians, all painted black, and "told him now they were friends, and presently he should goe to James towne, to send him two great gunnes, and a gryndstone, for which he would give him the Country of Capahowosick, and for ever esteeme him as his sonne Nantaquoud" (2:151). So much for making hatchets, bells, beads, and copper. But such changes (inconsistencies, if you will) are the stuff of reality.

Other explanations can be offered for the ostensible contradictions between the supposedly friendly Powhatan of *A True Relation* and the suspicious Powhatan of *The Generall Historie*. Perhaps Powhatan promised to free Smith but changed his mind. Or perhaps Powhatan intended from the first to adopt Smith after an initiation ceremony in which Pocahontas would sponsor him. Or perhaps at the trial the tribal leaders surprised Powhatan by arguing that the prisoner should be killed, and he tentatively agreed, only to have the pleadings of Pocahontas confirm his former decision. I concede, however, that it seems suspicious that Smith dropped Powhatan's early promise when retelling the story in *The Generall Historie*.

The Pocahontas Episode in Smith's Writings

Writers of personal narratives necessarily select details in reporting their experiences. The selection almost invariably imposes or emphasizes an interpretation of the experience.[11] Since the upshot of Smith's captivity was that Powhatan did not kill him and did let him return to Jamestown, I suspect that in *A True Relation* Smith unconsciously emphasized those details that made sense of the happy outcome. It would be natural to do so. But when he rewrote the account in 1624, he had had a number of subsequent dealings with Powhatan. He had learned by 1609 that Powhatan had killed the Roanoke colonists.[12] His view of Powhatan had changed, and consequently his interpretation of what happened during his captivity had also changed. Furthermore, the Pocahontas episode would not have seemed to him more important than several other occasions when his life was threatened during his captivity (he omitted another in *A True Relation*), and the Pocahontas episode was even a little embarrassing.

Moreover, *The Generall Historie* rewrites the events given in the 1612 tract *The Proceedings* rather than those in *A True Relation*. Powhatan's promise is not present in *The Proceedings*. There, Smith's entire captivity takes up only three sentences (1:213). After all, *The Proceedings* was compiled by Smith from the writings of others with Smith supplying materials to make the narrative a unified history. Unlike *A True Relation*, it was not a history of Smith's activities but a history of the colony. With *The Proceedings* by his elbow, Smith rewrote his Virginia adventures for *The Generall Historie* in much greater detail, but it never occurred to him to make his later retelling absolutely consistent with the account in *A True Relation*. Many details in *A True Relation* are not in *The Generall Historie* and vice versa. Smith had evidently forgotten and did not care what, exactly, he had written in the earliest Virginia tract. Liars have reason to try to be consistent. As I will show below, Smith was sometimes inconsistent within a single publication. He never tried to reconcile different versions of his Virginia experiences.

Wyndham Robertson and William Wirt Henry both suggested that Smith might have wanted to keep the Pocahontas incident a secret as long as he remained in Virginia.[13] They noted that Smith had been imprisoned for mutiny in 1607 on the way to Virginia and that his enemies, especially Edward Maria Wingfield, charged he had plotted to make himself king in Virginia (2:139). Of course the charge was nonsense, and Smith was restored to the council. Later Wingfield was tried for libeling Smith, found guilty, and fined two hundred pounds.[14] Nevertheless, a special relationship with Powhatan's favorite daughter would strengthen the anti-Smith faction's claim that he was plotting to become king. In his 1953 biography of Captain John Smith, Bradford Smith took up and advocated this possible explanation: "Smith had been close enough to a death sentence to know that if he were suspected of having some sort of intimate understanding with Powhatan's daughter, all the old rumors would begin to circulate again."[15] Robertson and Henry also pointed out that in September 1609, after Smith sustained his incapacitating burn, his enemies came to power and again charged him with wanting to become king in Virginia, now adding "by marrying Pocahontas, Powhatan's daughter" (1:274). Henry concluded: "it might well be that Smith thought it more prudent to say nothing of the matter, while he was under suspicion of plotting to make himself King of Virginia."[16]

William Wirt Henry suggested another reason why Smith might have suppressed the Pocahontas episode: "Smith was anxious to impress the colonists with the idea that he could control the Indians better than any one else, as his writings show, and he therefore had a motive for concealing the fact that he came near losing his life at the hands of their great King; and this motive might not only have prevented his talking of the rescue in Jamestown, but of writing concerning it to England."[17] Bradford Smith added a twist to this explanation:

> With his tenderness for his own reputation, particularly his reputation for bravery, he would have looked foolish coming into Jamestown with the tale that an Indian maiden had saved his life. Anyone who knows what an all-male community is like can imagine what remarks would have followed this admission. And even if Smith had been able to face the jibes at his supposed courage, he would have had to face an even more distasteful certainty—that the men would make leering remarks about his relations with the girl. Sex-starved themselves, they would never let the subject alone.[18]

As Robertson, Henry, and Bradford Smith argued, perhaps Smith deliberately suppressed the Pocahontas incident. But if Smith deliberately omitted it, I suspect he did so simply because it was embarrassing. He was, after all, among the most renowned soldiers of the day, famous for his feats at arms in eastern Europe. The references he later made to Pocahontas's saving him suggest that he was certainly not proud of the event. And the hypothesis that he deliberately omitted the Pocahontas episode might account for the more positive picture both of Powhatan and of the last part of Smith's captivity as related in *A True Relation*.

Smith may also simply have omitted the anecdote from his letter to a friend for no special reason. After all, Smith left out numerous other adventures that happened during the time covered by *A True Relation*. Then, when he wrote *The Gen-*

erall Historie, he related everything in greater detail. Indeed, *The Generall Historie* is a much fuller account of all Smith's Virginia adventures than the earlier reports of 1608 and 1612, adding dozens of details, escapades, and escapes from death, although, as I have pointed out, a few details present in *A True Relation* were omitted from the later, fuller version. Of course, all the other adventurous additions in *The Generall Historie* except those during Smith's captivity happened with white companions present and have never been challenged. Despite the numerous additions in *The Generall Historie*, many loose ends remain, and questions of interest to the reader are still unanswered.[19]

Deane, Robertson, Adams, and Henry all ignored Smith's remarkable accuracy in describing Virginia geography and the customs and religion of the Indians. Actually, Smith devoted comparatively little attention to his personal adventures in the Virginia tracts of 1608 and 1612, but he detailed with as much exactness as possible the route he traveled, the rivers he crossed, and the Indian rituals he witnessed. Smith's critics often condemn him for being vainglorious, but it is perfectly obvious in *A True Relation* and other accounts that he actually downplayed incidents when he was in danger and often omitted his own heroic actions.[20]

The brief account of his captivity in *The Proceedings* reported only one time when his life was in danger — when he was first captured. Smith, however, recorded three specific life-threatening situations in *A True Relation*: when he was first taken captive (1:45–47); when an Indian father tried to kill him in revenge as it became certain his young warrior son would die of a wound Smith inflicted (1:49); and when he was taken to the Topahanocke (Rappahannock) River for possible execution because he was suspected to be the captain of a ship that had, a year or two before, betrayed those Indians (1:51). *The Generall Historie* added two more events during his captivity when his life was threatened: the Pocahontas episode, and an incident shortly after he was first captured. Then, Smith was "tyed to a tree," and "as many as could stand about him prepared to shoot him, but the King holding up the Compass in his hand, they all laid downe their Bowes and Arrowes" (2:147). No one has ever expressed doubt that this incident occurred. Why not? Simply because it is unimportant to the later legends of Smith. But surely Smith could hardly have foreseen that being saved by Pocahontas was going to be any more important than this incident—or more important than numerous other times with white companions when he barely escaped death during his Virginia explorations.

There can be no doubt that Smith selectively reported his personal adventures in the letter that was published as *A True Relation*. The descriptions of Virginia's geography and obser-vations about Indian culture were much more important to his immediate audience and to Smith's purposes for writing than were his escapades. Smith not only omitted the Poca-hontas episode, but he also ignored the time he was tied to a tree and nearly shot; he overlooked his arrest in the Canary Islands for mutiny (cf. 1:98 n. 16; 2:139 n. 2); he did not men-tion the gallows prepared for him at "Mevis" (Nevis, Leeward Isles; 3:236); he neglected Wingfield's being tried and fined two hundred pounds for libeling him; and he left out being condemned to death on a trumped-up charge when he re-turned from his captivity, only to be saved by the arrival of Captain Christian Newport. (Smith only says that his enemies threatened to "depose him" from the council [1:61]; Wingfield reports he was to be executed.[21] Why claim that the Pocahontas story alone did not happen when none of these others are present in *A True Relation?* Why not say none of them happened — except the one confirmed by Wingfield? As Robertson wrote in 1860: "Now, what strikes one at the outset is, that this hypothesis [that Smith was lying when he claimed Pocahontas saved him] only removes one difficulty to create a greater; for it would seem easier to account for the omission in the first case, than for the imputed falsehood in the last."[22]

Charles Deane and Henry Adams mistakenly assumed that the Pocahontas episode was more important to Smith than other incidents when his life was threatened but preserved. It was only one event among many, but *A True Relation* was not primarily the story of his adventures. It described the discovery and exploration of Virginia and the rituals of the Virginia Indians. Only later writers, especially in the first half of the nineteenth century, made the Pocahontas episode famous.[23] Deane's and Adams's great anachronistic fallacy was to assume that the Smith-Pocahontas story dominated the history of Virginia's early settlement in the early seventeenth century as it dominated the imaginative history of Virginia's early settlement during the mid–nineteenth century. Nothing could be further from the truth. In fact, there is no good reason to expect to find the Pocahontas episode in *A True Relation*.

A Map and *The Proceedings*, 1612

Deane and Adams thought it incriminating that no reference to Pocahontas's saving Smith occurred in the two 1612 pamphlets, *A Map of Virginia* and *The Proceedings of the English Colonie in Virginia*. But such an account would have been out of place in *A Map of Virginia*. As the title page notes, *A Map* was devoted to "A Description of the Covntrey, The Commodities, People, Government and Religion." It did not deal with any of the adventures or explorations of Smith as such, though it recorded their geographical and ethnological results. Smith mentioned his captivity only in passing: "when Captaine Smith was their prisoner" (1:170).

As for *The Proceedings*, it told the story of Virginia from 1606 to 1612, three years after Smith left Virginia in October 1609. It was based on a number of writings by other people (1:197), though the whole was revised by Richard Pots, Smith, and William Symonds. In comparison with *A True Relation* or *The Generall Historie*, it contained little about Smith's adventures. The third chapter, where the captivity of Smith finds its chronological place, was evidently based upon writings by Anas Todkill, though Philip Barbour suggested that Nathaniel Powell might well have had a hand in the composition (1:195). Here is the entire account of Smith's captivity in *The Proceedings*:

> So he [Smith] had inchanted those poore soules (being their prisoner) in demonstrating unto them the roundnesse of the world, the course of the moone and starres, the cause of the day and night the largenes of the seas the quallities of our ships, shot and powder, The devision of the world, with the diversity of people, their complexions, customes and conditions. All which he fained to be under the command of Captaine Newport, whom he tearmed to them his father; of his arrival, it chanced he so directly prophecied, as they esteemed him an oracle; by these fictions he not only saved his owne life, and obtained his liberty, but had them at that command, he might command them what he listed. (1:215)

Whoever wrote it gave no details whatever about the captivity but only emphasized Smith's mastery of the Indians. Any relation of the several incidents when the Indians nearly killed him would certainly be out of place here. None of them are present. Why then expect to find a reference to the Pocahontas episode? It does not belong in *The Proceedings* any more than it does in *A Map of Virginia.*

Nevertheless, an allusion to the Pocahontas story occurs, I believe, in *A Map of Virginia.* Indeed, Henry Adams recognized that an oblique reference existed and attempted to discredit it. Smith devoted three chapters of *A Map* to observations on the Indians. In one passage, he described the capital punishments Powhatan inflicted. Smith gave three methods. The first was to "cast the offenders to broyle to death" into a pit filled with flaming charcoal (1:174). When William Strachey reprinted the passage in his *Historie of Travell into Virginia Britania,* he added that it occurred "at what tyme Capt. Smith was Prysoner with them, and to the sight whereof, Capt. Smith for some purpose was brought." Since we know from Strachey's other references that he consulted Smith personally, cited his conversations, and praised him, there is no reason to doubt that Smith told him that he saw this execution during his captivity.[24]

Smith thus described the second method of execution: "Sometimes he [Powhatan] causeth the heads of them that offend him, to be laid upon the altar or sacrificing stone, and one with clubbes beates out their braines" (1:174–75). This procedure recapitulated what was happening to Smith when Pocahontas saved him. Perhaps he saw an execution carried out in this manner, but no record of it exists. Smith learned this method, I believe, during the Pocahontas episode. In the third method an enemy was bound to a tree: "The executioner cutteth off his joints one after another, ever casting what they cut off into the fire; then doth he proceed with shels and reeds to case the skinne from his head and face; then doe they rip

his belly and so burne him with the tree and all. Thus themselves reported they executed George Cassen" (1:175). Cassen
was one of the persons whom Smith left behind with the barge
when he went exploring further upstream by canoe. Smith evidently learned all three methods of execution during his captivity, and the second describes what he thought was about to
happen to him when Pocahontas saved him.[25] To be sure, it is
not a direct reference, but it should mitigate the argument that
neither Smith nor his companions referred to the Pocahontas
story before it appeared in the revised edition of *New Englands
Trials* in 1622.

Henry Adams tried to use the reference to discredit Smith.
He wrote:

> There is in the text which accompanies the Map only one
> passage that bears upon the point now principally in dispute.
> Among the customs which he describes as peculiar to the Indi-
> ans was the form of execution practiced against criminals. Their
> heads, he says, were placed upon an altar, or sacrificing-stone,
> while 'one with clubbes beates out their braines.' During his
> captivity, he adds, not indeed that he had actually seen this mode
> of execution, but that an Indian had been beaten in his presence
> till he fell senseless, without a cry or complaint. Here we have,
> therefore, the whole idea of the story which he afterwards made
> public.[26]

Actually, Smith gave three examples of how Powhatan was
"very terrible and tyrannous in punishing such as offend him"
(2:174). Beating out the brains of the offender was the second of three methods of capital punishment. After describing
the three, Smith wrote: "Their ordinary correction is to beate
them with cudgels. Wee have seene a man kneeling on his
knees, and at Powhatans command, two men have beat him

on the bare skin, till he hath fallen senseless in a sound, and yet never cry nor complained" (2:175). Though approximately ninety words separates the two accounts in Smith, Adams runs them together. Moreover, there is surely a difference between a man whose head is laid upon "the altar or sacrificing stone" while his brains are beaten out and a man kneeling on his knees while being beaten unconscious. Smith gave the first as one of three examples of execution; the second was the "ordinary" Indian punishment. Adams, I fear, deliberately misrepresented Smith. As I will show in chapter 3, Adams revised and added to this argument in the 1891 version of his essay, but the addition only further discredits him.

No one should be surprised that the Pocahontas episode is not set forth at length in either *A Map of Virginia* or *The Proceedings*. It does not belong in the 1612 tracts. An indirect reference, however, to the Pocahontas episode does seem to be present in *A Map of Virginia*. Adams evidently realized that, contrary to the assertion of Charles Deane, an allusion existed in *A Map*. Perhaps that was part of the reason he at first rejected Palfrey's suggestion that Smith lied.[27] But when he wrote the essay, Adams tried as best he could to discount the indirect evidence found in *A Map*.

The Letter to Queen Anne, 1616

Smith directly referred eight times to Pocahontas's saving him. Adams and Henry only deal with three: the 1616 letter to Queen Anne, the second edition of *New Englands Trials*, and the main account in *The Generall Historie*. Chronologically, the first reference occurred in Smith's 1616 letter to Queen Anne. The letter was not published at the time, but Smith printed it in his *Generall Historie*. There he tells us that "before" Pocahontas "arrived in London" (evidently after she arrived in Plymouth, England, on June 3, 1616), he sought to make "her qualities knowne to the Queene's most excellent Majestie and her Court" (2:258) and therefore wrote a letter concerning her to Queen Anne.[28] In the letter, Smith mentioned his capture by the Indians: "After some six weeks fatting amongst those Salvage Courtiers, at the minute of my execution, she hazarded the beating out of her owne braines to save mine, and not only that, but so prevailed with her father that I was safely conducted to James towne" (2:259).

Because of Smith's letter to the queen, Henry Adams could not at first accept John Gorham Palfrey's suggestion that the Smith-Pocahontas episode was a lie. Adams wrote Palfrey on October 23, 1861, about "what graveled me most in the search after doubts":

> I find in Smith's book published at all events as early as 1625, his letter introducing her to the Queen, and in this letter he restates all the facts about Pocahontas and distinctly says that she saved his life by throwing herself over him just as the executioner was going to strike. Now could Smith have asserted this if Pocahontas herself, and through her of course her husband, had been able to brand it at once as a fiction? Smith details his own interview with her in England and to my mind it bears the strongest marks of truth. She seems to have been then at least nearly a stranger to him. She had not seen him for near ten years when she was still a child. Everyone who talked with her (and she talked English) must have mentioned this exploit of hers, and she could have had no motive to keep up the falsehood, if it was one. She was notorious enough without it, and seems to have been a sombre, silent, reflective, Indian sort of being hardly up to such a deceit. Her father too still lived and long conversations of his with English people are extant. We do not hear that

he ever denied Smith's story which must have been repeated to him, one would think.[29]

But the weight of the combined authority of Palfrey and Charles Deane, who replied to Palfrey's letter and indirectly to Adams's, caused Adams to change his mind. Deane pointed out that "the letter which he [Smith] says he wrote to Queene Anne, in 1616," was first published in *The Generall Historie*. "Perhaps Smith wrote it. I should be very sorry to suppose he did not. Pocahontas, Queene Anne and Powhatan were all in their graves, before Smith's story was ever in print."[30]

In his 1860 edition of Wingfield, Charles Deane had discounted the reference to the Pocahontas episode in Smith's letter to Queen Anne by saying that he "intimated" the story to her "in general terms." Deane's 1862 reviewer, however, pointed out that Smith in fact "gave quite a circumstantial explicit detail of" the Pocahontas story. He quoted the letter, stated that if it had "been false and fabulous, Rolfe and Pocahontas were present to contradict it." And he asked the commonsensical (and, I think, the unanswerable) question, "What imaginable motive can be assigned for Smith's jeopardying his character at court, by fabricating a story redounding only to the honor of Pocahontas?"[31]

Repeating Deane's letter to him, Adams argued in 1867 that since no copy of the letter was known from 1616, either Smith did not write it then or the original letter contained no reference to his being saved by Pocahontas. Adams charged that Smith made up the letter and/or its Pocahontas episode when he published it in *The Generall Historie*. Adams explained: "At the time when it was published, in 1624, not only had Pocahontas been long dead, but Queen Anne herself had, in 1619, followed her to the grave, and Smith remained alone to tell his own story." Revising the essay in 1871, Adams rather lamely added that "the Virginia Company had no interest in denying the truth of a story so well calculated to draw popular sympathy toward the colony."[32]

William Wirt Henry found Adams's attempt to discredit Smith's letter to Queen Anne absurdly weak. He pointed out that though the queen had died, King James was still alive in 1624. Moreover, he said, "Prince Charles was familiar with the matter. The Rev. Samuel Purchas . . . was alive, and indeed, unless we are to suppose some strange mortality had befallen the court, it must have been that most of the persons who constituted it in 1616 were alive in 1624."[33] Henry concluded his rebuttal:

So that to maintain his argument Mr. Adams asks us to believe that Smith in his "General Historie," published in 1624, not only published a falsehood as to his rescue by Pocahontas in 1608, which his companions in Virginia, who still survived, and some of whom were in England, would detect instantly; but, as if for fear it would not be readily detected in this way, coupled it with a falsehood, or falsehoods, as to what had happened in England in 1616, which last he knew would be certainly detected by many persons still alive in England. This would seem strange, indeed, for a man putting a falsehood into history, but it is not more remarkable than the fact that he was not detected by any of his contemporaries; and for two hundred and fifty years, as it were in spite of himself, he has deceived the world. Really, the tax Mr. Adams imposes upon our credulity has become quite oppressive.[34]

I completely agree with William Wirt Henry. It strains one's credulity to believe that Smith in 1624 would lie about a letter written to the queen eight years before. Numerous persons who had befriended Pocahontas when she was in England in 1616/17, like Dr. Theodore Goulston (1572–1632), would have known the truth. Though John Rolfe died in 1622, his brother Henry Rolfe (who took under his care Pocahontas's infant, Thomas Rolfe) and the entire Virginia circle, as well as the entire court circle, must have known about a letter to the queen. Samuel Purchas (1577–1626) knew both the entire group of Virginia colonists and the court circle. Further, he had numerous interviews during 1616 and 1617 with Pocahontas, Uttamatomakkin and his wife, Matachauna (Pocahontas's sister), and the dozen or so other Indians who came to London through an interpreter he identified as "Sir Thomas Dale's man."

Henry said that Prince Charles "was familiar" with the letter but did not say why; evidently he thought it was simply because Charles was a member of the court. The date that Dale, Rolfe, Pocahontas, Uttamatomakkin, and others arrived from Virginia at Plymouth was the same date that Captain John Smith's *Description of New England* was entered in the Stationers' Register (1:369). Both events occurred on June 3, 1616. On June 18, Humfrey Lownes finished printing *A Description* and added that date at the end (1:361). By that time, over two weeks after Dale and his party arrived at Plymouth, Smith, who was in London, must have learned that Pocahontas was in England. It is not known when, exactly, Smith presented *A Description of New England* to Prince Charles, the dedicatee, but common sense says that it would have been as soon after the book was printed as possible. Therefore Captain John Smith must have had an audience with Prince Charles shortly after June 18, 1616. Prince Charles, who was asked in the dedication "to change" the "Barbarous" Indian place-names for "English" ones (1:309), did so. A leaf with Prince Charles's changes was printed and added to the book (1:319). It is only reasonable to suppose that Smith presented his letter to Queen Anne about Pocahontas at the same time that he appeared at court to give a copy of his map and *A Description of New England* to Prince Charles.

William Herbert (1580–1630), earl of Pembroke, who became a member of the Virginia Council and invested four hundred pounds in the Virginia Company while Smith was president in Virginia, was lord chamberlain from December 23, 1615, to 1625.[35] He is among the many persons in the court circle who must have known of the 1616 letter and who lived until well after the appearance of *The Generall Historie*. As lord chamberlain, he would have set the time for the presentation of Pocahontas and Uttamatomakkin to James I and would have been in charge at the actual ceremony. He knew whatever happened at court. Like James I, William Herbert must have known of Smith's letter to Queen Anne. With a keen interest in colonization, he probably read all of Smith's writings about Virginia and New England. He was made a member of the council for New England in 1620 and, that same year, patented thirty thousand Virginia acres.[36] Smith dedicated his *True Travels* to Herbert in 1630. If Smith had lied about his letter to the queen in 1616 or about Pocahontas's saving him, Herbert would have known it. Smith would not have dared to dedicate his *True Travels* to Herbert if Herbert knew or even suspected Smith to be lying.

If Smith had lied about the letter, King James (1566–1625), Prince Charles (1600–1649), Lord Pembroke (d. 1630), Samuel Purchas (1577–1626), and many others would have known it. If we are to think that Smith lied and made up the story of his letter or that he changed its contents, then we must believe that numerous people in the court circle and in the Virginia Company circle conspired in the lie. The supposition that John

Smith did not write the 1616 letter or that it did not contain the Pocahontas episode involves so many of his contemporaries in lies, conspiracies, silences, and deceits that no unbiased person who considers the evidence could doubt its truth. As William Wirt Henry pointed out, most members of the court circle in 1616 were still alive and well in 1624. Henry Adams should have known this when he initially wrote his propaganda. He certainly realized it after W. W. Henry pointed it out. Yet he persevered in his untenable position in the last revision of his essay in 1891.

If we had no other references to the Pocahontas story, Smith's letter to Queen Anne alone would prove that Pocahontas had, "at the minute of my execution, . . . hazarded the beating out of her owne braines to save mine" (2:259).

New Englands Trials, 1622

Smith directly referred to Pocahontas's saving his life for the second time (but the first published) in the revised edition of *New Englands Trials* in 1622. Adams, echoing Charles Deane, tried to discredit this account (though, to be sure, Adams's attack is merely an *argumentum ad hominem* and has nothing to do, logically, with the Pocahontas episode) by claiming that Smith here invented the cowardice of two of his men. Adams wrote that the 1622 account "is, we are sorry to say it, more certainly mendacious than any of the rest. Read it in whatever light we please, it is creditable neither to Smith's veracity nor to his sense of honor." Adams maintained that Smith unjustly charged John Robinson and Thomas Emry, the two men who had gone upriver in a canoe with him and whom he had left when he went off with his Indian guide, with cowardice. "To throw upon the invented cowardice of companions who were far away, out of sight and out of hearing of the contest, the blame for a disaster that was solely due to his own over-boldness, was not an honorable way of dealing with his command."[37] William Wirt Henry, however, completely discredited Deane and Adams by proving that they simply confused Smith's allusion. Smith referred "to the men at the barge, and not to Robinson and Emery" at the canoe. Lured by Indian maidens, three men at the barge disobeyed Smith's orders and went ashore.[38] Surprised by warriors, the men fled without firing their weapons. One man, George Cassen, was captured. Smith was disgusted with the three for disobeying his orders and going ashore and especially with the two who fled, abandoning Cassen. They should have fought and retreated to the barge with Cassen. Of course Cassen, under torture, told the Indians that Smith had gone further upstream in a canoe with two companions (Robinson and Emry) and two Indian guides. So the Indians went after them, killed Robinson and Emry by the canoe and set out after Smith and his guide. In proving that Smith did not, in fact, censure Robinson and Emry, W. W. Henry showed that both Charles Deane and Henry Adams were careless, if not overeager and partisan, in condemning Smith. Reprinting his essay "Captain John Smith" in 1891, Henry Adams again thoroughly revised its prose style and, in a number of places, also revised its content. He realized that William Wirt Henry had caught him in an outright error and silently dropped the charges that the 1622 account was "more certainly mendacious" and "creditable neither to Smith's veracity nor to his sense of honor."[39] Adams's deletion left him with nothing to say about Smith's 1622 account. He quietly ignored it in the 1891 revision.

William Wirt Henry, who did not have a copy of Smith's

New Englands Trials but knew it from the reprinting in Purchas's *Hakluytus Posthumus*, mistakenly thought that Smith wrote it from New England. Henry's arguments in favor of the truthfulness of the episode as recorded in *New Englands Trials* are nevertheless devastating. Henry pointed out that Smith called upon specific witnesses to his treatment of Opechancanough: "Them two honorable Gentlemen (Captaine George Percie and Captaine Francis West), two of the Phittiplaces, and some other such noble gentlemen and resolute spirits bore their shares with me, and now living in England, did see me take the murdering Opechankanough now their great King by the long lock on his head, with my pistole at his breast, I led him among his greatest forces." Smith conceded, however, that he was not always so heroic, and in this context he mentions, for the first time in print, the Pocahontas incident: "It is true that in our greatest extremitie they shot me, slue three of my men, and by the folly of them that fled took me prisoner; yet God made Pocahontas the King's daughter the means to deliver me: and thereby taught mee to know their trecheries to preserve the rest" (1:432). Henry commented:

> From this it appears that Smith, in a letter published in 1622, called upon four persons by name, as witnesses of a certain act which he had performed in Virginia which showed his power over the Indians, but acknowledges that they once took him prisoner, and would have slain him had not Pocahontas saved him. Had this last been a fabrication of Smith, it certainly would have been so recognized by these witnesses, who had been with him in Virginia and had often seen Pocahontas. It seems incredible that Smith in New England should have referred to these gentlemen in England, as witnesses of one statement in his letter, and immediately followed it with a statement they would certainly recognize as false.[40]

I find Henry's argument fully convincing, even without considering, as I shall show in chapter 3, that George Percy and Francis West were by then Smith's enemies and would have wanted to discredit him.

Further, the historical context surrounding the publication of *New Englands Trials* deserves consideration. After learning of the Indians' massacre of the Virginia whites, Smith reissued *New Englands Trials*, which he had first published in 1620, with some additions that asserted his willingness and competence to undertake retribution against the Indians. Opechancanough, Powhatan's younger brother and now the overlord of the Powhatan confederacy, had organized and led the massacre. Smith's tract told how he had controlled the Indians when he was in Virginia and in particular how he had handled Opechancanough when that chief sought to kill him. Smith's purpose for reprinting and revising *New Englands Trials* was to advertise himself as an expert Indian fighter. There was no reason for him to allude to the Pocahontas episode except that others knew about it and might cite it to detract from his reputation. Evidently Percy, West, Michael and William Fettiplace, and others all knew that story—in addition to the accounts of Smith's heroic exploits against Opechancanough. Therefore Smith thought himself obliged to mention it. The way Smith brought up the episode in 1622 ("It is true . . .") strongly suggests that he was rather ashamed of it.

But let us suppose for a minute that the naysayers are right. Having just asserted his extraordinary ability as an Indian fighter against the great Indian chief Opechancanough and having just specifically called upon four old Virginia hands present in London, and others not individually named, to examine and testify to the truth of his statements, he then makes up a lie (for the first time in print) that portrays himself as a helpless victim of the Indians. The supposition is ridiculous. The only reasonable conclusion is that the Pocahontas episode happened and that Smith's Virginia contemporaries knew about it. In alluding to the Pocahontas episode, Smith was trying to forestall criticism of his prowess by conceding that he had been captured and, later, freed by the interposition of Pocahontas.

If we had no reference to the Pocahontas story other than the brief allusion in *New Englands Trials*, that alone would prove to any impartial judge that "God made Pocahontas the King's daughter the means to deliver me" (1:432).

The 1623 References

Smith twice referred to the Pocahontas episode in 1623. In May or early June he testified before the commissioners appointed by King Charles I to inquire into the Virginia Company's supposed irregularities.[41] The commissioners, Sir William Jones, Sir Nicholas Fortescue, Sir Francis Gofton, Sir Richard Sutton, Sir William Pitt, Sir Henry Bourchier, and Sir Henry Spiller, constituted a number of England's most experienced administrators.[42] They knew personally many members of the Virginia Company and spent six to eight weeks gathering testimony concerning the company's affairs. According to Wesley Frank Craven, they conducted a "thorough investigation" into the history and state of the Virginia Company.[43] During the course of his sworn testimony before the commissioners, Smith said: "Six weeks I was led captive by those Barbarians, though some of my men were slaine, and the rest fled, yet it pleased God to make their great King's daughter the means to returne me safe to James towne" (2:323).

Smith told no details about how Pocahontas saved him, and

certainly a long account of his captivity and of being saved various times would have been out of place in his testimony, but the gist of the statement was clear. Pocahontas had in some way saved him during his captivity. Since the commissioners summoned before them numerous former Virginia colonists present in London and all the leading members of the Virginia Company during their sustained, minute examination of the company's affairs, it does not make sense that Smith would lie to them about a personal experience in Virginia. The lie would have been immediately exposed. Only someone imagining a conspiracy by Smith, the former Virginia colonists (friends and enemies), the leading members of the Virginia Company, and the commissioners can think Smith lied during his testimony. To be sure, his statements were not published at the time, but they would have been widely known. And Smith printed his testimony just one year later in *The Generall Historie*. Adams ignored the reference, but William Wirt Henry added it as an additional reason for believing that Pocahontas saved Smith when he recast his 1875 article into his 1882 lecture.[44]

In the fall of 1623 Smith published the broadside prospectus for his *Generall Historie*. Outlining the events to be discussed in the third book, Smith noted: "Powhatan entertained him, would have slaine him, and his daughter saved his life" (2:11). Since the broadside was practically unknown in the nineteenth century, neither Adams nor Henry mentioned it.[45]

If we had no reference to the Smith-Pocahontas story other than Smith's testimony before the commissioners in 1623, we would positively know that Pocahontas had been "the means to returne me safe to James towne" (2:323).

The Generall Historie, 1624

In *The Generall Historie of Virginia*, Smith referred to the Pocahontas episode for the fifth, sixth, and seventh times. Dedicating the book to Frances Howard, he cataloged Pocahontas as the third of four foreign ladies who befriended him:

> Yet my comfort is, that heretofore honorable and vertuous Ladies, and comparable but amongst themselves, have offred me rescue and protection in my greatest dangers: even in forraine parts, I have felt reliefe from that sex. The beauteous Lady Tragabigzanda, when I was a slave to the Turkes, did all she could to secure me. When I overcame the Bashaw of Nalbrits in Tartaria, the charitable Lady Callamata supplyed my necessities. In the utmost of many extremities, that blessed Pokahontas, the great Kings daughter of Virginia, oft saved my life. When I escaped the crueltie of Pirats and most furious stormes, a long time alone in a small Boat at Sea, and driven ashore in France, the good Lady Madam Chanoyes, bountifully assisted me. (2:41–42)

Though Adams and Henry both ignored this reference, Charles Deane had noticed it, and in 1866 he tried to discredit Smith with it. Others had earlier spoken of Smith's chivalric ideals, generally in praise, and called him a knight errant.[46] Deane, however, was the first to impugn him for his chivalric imagination: "Smith was a true knight errant, and was always ready to go down on his knees to the fair sex, and to confess the obligations he owed to many famous ladies." Then Deane quoted the above passage. Deane implied that Smith either made up or exaggerated all his supposed debts to women.[47] It is the only Deane attack on Smith that Adams chose not to amplify. But Adams completed his Smith article early in 1862, before Deane's 1866 edition of *A True Relation* appeared, though Adams added some material to the article and revised it in 1866.[48] Perhaps Adams overlooked Deane's attack, or perhaps he thought, as I do, that the implied charge against Smith was too weak to repeat. If Smith had not praised them, three of the four "famous ladies" would be completely unknown. Or perhaps Adams did not want to mention a fourth time that Smith referred to the Pocahontas episode.

The second allusion in *The Generall Historie* to the Pocahontas episode occurs in the table of contents (2:54), which repeats the 1623 outline. The third and longest account appears in Book 3. It is the classic story, yet even here Smith almost seems to gloss over it. Jay B. Hubbell commented that if Smith invented the story, it was "strange that in his final and fullest account of this extraordinary scene he gave the rescue only part of one long and formless sentence in a folio volume of 248 pages." Hubbell added, "If the Captain had expected this incident to be better remembered than any other of his many substantial achievements and thrilling adventures, surely he would have expanded and embroidered this bare outline of a great romantic episode."[49]

In fact, I believe that the Pocahontas episode was still a little embarrassing for Smith. He included it in 1624, seven years after the death of Pocahontas, in part simply because he was telling the Virginia adventures in greater detail and in part to celebrate Pocahontas. Like many of his former friends and old companions, she had died, and the memory of her life and deeds was fading. Everett Emerson perceptively pointed out that several additions to Book 3 of *The Generall Historie* "served as a memorial treatment of Pocahontas, the dead wife of John Rolfe [also dead by 1624], whose bravery and devotion to the English Smith emphasized."[50] Here is *The Generall Historie* account:

At his [Smith's] entrance before the King [Powhatan], all the people gave a great shout. The Queene of Appamatuck was appointed to bring him water to wash his hands, and another brought him a bunch of feathers, in stead of a Towell to dry them: having feasted him after their best barbarous manner they could, a long consultation was held, but the conclusion was, two great stones were brought before Powhatan: then as many as could layd hands on him, dragged him to them, and thereon laid his head, and being ready with their clubs, to beate out his braines, Pocahontas the Kings dearest daughter, when no intreaty could prevaile, got his head in her armes, and laid her owne upon his to save him from death: whereat the Emperour was contented he should live to make him hatchets, and her bells, beads, and copper; for they thought him as well of all occupations as themselves. For the King himselfe will make his owne robes, shooes, bowes, arrowes, pots; plant, hunt, or doe any thing so well as the rest. (2:150–51)

The episode was certainly not a heroic performance by Smith, and he evidently saw no good reason, in a life full of high adventure and hairbreadth escapes from death, to dwell upon it. He could not know that it would become, in the words of Henry Adams, "the most romantic episode in the whole history of his country." [51]

Following Deane, Adams charged that the addition of the Pocahontas episode in *The Generall Historie* was consistent with Smith's usual vainglorious practice. Adams said that when Smith revised and rewrote the account of his captivity in *The Generall Historie*, "his own share in the affairs of the Colony is magnified at the expense of all his companions." Adams gave several supposed instances.[52] Adams's first discrepancy was that Smith said in *A True Relation* that eight Indians ordinarily guarded him, but in *The Generall Historie* he wrote that the

Indians took him to "a long house, where thirtie or fortie tall fellows did guard him" (2:148). Henry replied that the thirty or forty guards were present only at first and that later only eight guarded him.[53] That there were sometimes more and sometimes fewer guards seems only reasonable to me.

Second, Adams found that Smith said in *A True Relation* that he was served more venison than ten men could devour and in *The Generall Historie* that he was brought more bread and venison than would have served twenty men. Henry attempted to refute the discrepancy by concentrating upon Smith's exact diction, but I think both arguments are rather silly, as I will point out below.

Third, Adams noted that in *A True Relation* Smith reported that at the end of his captivity Powhatan sent him back to Jamestown with four men, "one that usually carried my Gowne and Knapsacke after me, two other loded with bread, and one to accompanie me" (1:57). But in *The Generall Historie* Smith said that he was sent to Jamestown "with 12 guides" (2:151). Henry replied that of the four mentioned in the first account, "three carried burdens, and one was at Smith's side to obey his commands, while the other eight or twelve . . . guided or guarded him to Jamestown."[54]

Neither Adams nor Henry mentioned a number of other differences between the accounts. The three versions in *A True Relation*, *The Proceedings*, and *The Generall Historie* contain discrepancies regarding what the Indians were going to bring back. *A True Relation* says that when Powhatan next saw Smith, "with a merrie countenance he asked me for certaine peeces which I promised him, when I went to Paspahegh. I told [him] according to my promise, that I proffered the man that went with me foure Demy Culverings [cannon each weighing approximately four thousand pounds], in that he so desired a great

Gunne, but they refused to take them; whereat with a lowde laughter, he desired [me] to give him some of lesse burthen, as for the other I gave him them, being sure that none could carrie them" (1:65). *The Proceedings* says: "Powhatan having sent with this Captaine divers of his men loaded with provision, he had conditioned, and so appointed his trustie messengers to bring but 2 or 3 of our great ordenances, but the messengers being satisfied with the sight of one of them discharged, ran away amazed with feare, till meanes was used with guifts to asure them our loves" (1:213). And *The Generall Historie* says that after a ceremony with the medicine men, unmentioned in previous accounts, "then Powhatan more like a devill then a man with some two hundred more as blacke as himselfe, came unto him [Smith] and told him now they were friends, and presently he should goe to James towne, to send him two great gunnes, and a gryndstone, for which he would give him the Country of Capahowosick, and for ever esteeme him as his sonne Nantaquoud" (2:151). Was it four cannons, two or three cannons, or two cannons and a grindstone? Twelve men seems like a much more reasonable number than four to try to bring back even two cannons and a grindstone, though the argument is moot. Obviously Smith, who wrote with *The Proceedings* beside him, did not care whether it was two cannons or four, a grindstone or not. And he did not begin to think that his readers would care.

Adams provided other examples that have nothing to do with the captivity account, but he and Deane were wrong in generalizing that Smith, in retelling the story of his Virginia adventures in *The Generall Historie*, made himself invariably more heroic. Alexander Brown seized upon and repeated the charge, citing one example.[55] But Jarvis Morse pointed out that sometimes Smith made himself seem more heroic, sometimes he made himself seem less heroic, often he made others more heroic—my favorite example is the account of Anas Todkill's saving the exploring expedition at the risk of his life (2:173–74)—but most often he simply added more correct information and more detail that had nothing to do with the actions of himself or others.[56]

Adams and Henry both applied a standard of accuracy and documentation to Smith's account that he and his contemporaries would have thought unimportant and foolish. Perhaps the best single example of Smith's disregard for exact accuracy in reporting what happened to him occurred in *The Generall Historie* when he told of his first being captured. In one paragraph he said that two hundred Indians attacked him and he killed two of them (2:146). In the very next paragraph he said that three hundred Indians attacked him and he killed three (2:146–47). If the two hundred figure had appeared in *A True Relation* and the three hundred figure in *The Generall Historie*, Henry Adams would surely have seized upon the discrepancy as a splendid example of Smith's later exaggeration.

Smith, however, obviously did not know whether two or three hundred Indians beset him. Dozens and dozens and dozens and dozens of Indians were assaulting him. He fired at them and killed or wounded two and probably more. Who knew exactly? Furthermore, we cannot know if he meant to include in the number he killed those whom he wounded at the time who subsequently died. Since Smith knew that at least two Indians died later of wounds received in capturing him, it seems possible that Smith underestimates, rather than exaggerates, the number he killed. And I should point out that he mentioned the death of the second Indian only in his earliest publication, *A True Relation*. It is not in the revised and expanded *Generall Historie*.[57]

The mapmaker Smith thought it was important to be accurate about geography, but neither he nor anyone else in his time cared whether the amount of food would feed ten or twenty men. It was an immense amount of food! When Smith writes that "thirtie or fortie tall fellows did guard him" (2:148), it is obvious that he does not think it important whether the number was thirty or forty—or forty-one or twenty-nine! There were lots of guards! Who was counting? Not Smith. And he didn't think his readers would. Why would they?

I am making two related points. The first is that readers and writers did not expect exact accuracy concerning such matters in the Renaissance and seventeenth century. The second is that Smith never once thought anyone seriously doubted the basic truth of what he reported.

As Wyndham Robertson pointed out in 1860, books of travel in the Renaissance and seventeenth century characteristically had "some garniture of extravagance and liberal embellishment." Nevertheless, Robertson went on to say that he did "not remember an instance of any confutation, or contradiction, of any important fact stated by him [Smith]; while instances of confirmation are innumerable." Henry David Thoreau loved the "reckless, hit or miss" style of the earliest American writers. He praised them for caring "more to speak heartily than scientifically true." A modern scholar of Renaissance literature, William Jewkes, has argued that the popular vogue of the romance influenced all travel literature of the Renaissance and that "it is the clear influence of the romantic mode of viewing experience which best entitles these travel accounts to the label of literature." The chivalric romance influenced Smith, just as it did all other Renaissance writers. But that does not mean that Smith lied; he merely saw his experiences through glasses tinted by the zeitgeist of the times.[58]

The rise of history as a supposedly exact or scientific study in the nineteenth century changed readers' attitudes. Indeed, Henry Adams has been described as "the first of the scientific school of American historians." Such supposed objectivity is, we know, impossible. Or perhaps I should say that, except among some quantitative historians, it is no longer so fashionable to believe in "scientific" history.[59] Adams, however, presumably thought absolute objectivity and accuracy possible. His point of view was anachronistic and false, particularly regarding Elizabethan and Jacobean literature.

My second point is that the very inconsistencies between the versions of the captivity prove that no one doubted Smith. Since Smith, in telling and in retelling the tale, chose to report what he recalled as he wrote rather than to incorporate and expand an earlier version, he obviously never dreamed that anyone doubted the details of his Virginia adventures. He had no reason to try to be absolutely consistent. He retold the escapades the way he remembered them later, adding as many further details as he could recall, partly to make the record as full and as correct as he could, partly to make the story of early Virginia more understandable, partly to make the account more interesting (he was becoming a better writer), and partly to memorialize his former companions who had perished.

Henry Adams followed up a line of thought suggested by John Gorham Palfrey and speculated, "It is not even necessary to suppose that Smith himself invented the additions to his original story." Adams suggested that "the mere exercise of the popular imagination, attracted by a wild and vivid picture of savage life" might be the real origin of the Pocahontas episode. He further thought that "hack writers" might have "adapted his story for popular effect" and embodied it in a play. He concluded that Smith "may have merely accepted them [the additions found in *The Generall Historie*] after they had obtained a strong and general hold on the minds of his contemporaries."[60] Frankly, I find these suggestions absurd.[61] Anyone who has critically considered the nature of the revisions in *The Generall Historie*—most are factual, either correcting mistakes or giving fuller information—must regard Adams's speculations with astonished disbelief.

William Wirt Henry's comments on *The Generall Historie* emphasized Smith's reputation for truthfulness among his contemporaries, especially citing the opinion of Samuel Purchas and the fact that Purchas reprinted the Pocahontas episode in 1625. Henry, however, weakened his arguments by saying that Smith wrote *The Generall Historie* "at the request of the Virginia Company, and of course it had their approval," and further by saying that it was "prepared at their request and largely from materials in their office."[62] Smith used the company's publications, of which he evidently had a collection, and probably borrowed some materials from Purchas, but the reference Henry cited (*CW* 2:237–39) suggests he may have confused an account by Lord De La Warr with a writing by Smith. Indeed, Purchas himself wrote in 1625 that Smith was "no reputed favourite or favourer of that Society [the Virginia Company] and their actions."[63]

Henry further weakened his case when he stated that Smith's account was "made openly and repeatedly, where it could have been contradicted by Pocahontas and others cognizant of the fact, had it been untrue."[64] Though one might like to think that Henry was referring to Smith's letter to Queen Anne of 1616, he had been discussing *The Generall Historie* of 1624. Pocahontas and Rolfe, who died in early 1622, of course, were both dead before the Smith-Pocahontas episode first appeared in print in late 1622. At best, Henry's last point is confusing. Nevertheless, evidence from Smith's contemporaries, especially Purchas, is as I shall argue in chapter 3, a key reason for believing that the Pocahontas episode must be truthful.

Frances Mossiker echoed Henry concerning the evidence from contemporaries in asserting that the Smith-Pocahontas episode took place. She pointed out that six old Virginia hands were back in London when *The Generall Historie* appeared in 1624: Captain Samuel Argall, Ralph Hamor, Sir George Percy, Michael and William Fettiplace, and David Wiffin. She added that Percy replied to some of Smith's statements in *The Generall Historie* but said nothing about the Pocahontas episode. She concluded: "Smith's account of his rescue at the hands of Pocahontas stood unrefuted, in 1624, by Percy or by any other of the several First Planters and veterans of the First or Second Supply known to have returned from Virginia to London at that time." [65]

If we had no other reference to Pocahontas's saving Smith except the key one describing what happened during his captivity, we nevertheless would positively know that Pocahontas had "when no intreaty could prevaile, got his head in her armes, and laid her owne upon his to save him from death: whereat the Emperour was contented he should live" (2:151).

The True Travels, 1630

The eighth and last time Smith referred to Pocahontas's saving his life was in *The True Travels*, the story of the adventures of his youth. Near the end of the book, he recapitulated "how he was taken prisoner by the Savages, by the King of *Pamaunke* tied to a tree to be shot to death, led up and downe their Country to be shewed for a wonder; fatted as he thought, for a sacrifice for their Idoll, before whom they conjured him three dayes, with strange dances and invocations; then brought him before their Emperor *Powhatan*, that commanded him to be slaine; how his daughter *Pocahontas* saved his life . . . you may read at large in his general history of *Virginia*, the *Summer Iles*, and *New England*" (3:237, 238). Evidently in the six years between the publication of *The Generall Historie* and *The True Travels* no one had challenged Smith's account of Pocahontas's saving his life. If someone had, he would hardly have cited it in his autobiography featuring his early adventures.

Indeed, both William Herbert, earl of Pembroke (a dedicatee of *The True Travels*) and Robert Bruce Cotton, the great authority on English history and collector of manuscripts, belonged to the Virginia Company, knew many of the colonists who returned to England, and would have been told about Smith's lies—if he had lied in his previous works.[66] Certainly Cotton, who asked Smith to write the story of his early adventures in Europe, must have known and believed the later American ones. And it is unthinkable that Lord Pembroke, who had been lord chamberlain in 1616, would have allowed *The True Travels* to be dedicated to him if Smith had been regarded as a liar. Further, in a dedicatory poem to *The True Travels*, Richard Brathwait, a prolific minor poet, alluded to the Pocahontas episode (3:145).[67]

The True Travels features the event in Smith's life of which he was most proud and the great triumph that he thought others might not believe—the three duels to the death that Smith fought in single combat as the Christian champion. That was the high point of his military career. His slightly later contemporary Thomas Fuller skeptically remarked about Smith's Balkan and Middle Eastern adventures, "The scene whereof is laid at such a distance, they are cheaper credited than confuted."[68] Smith cared greatly that his early adventures be believed. I suspect that by 1616 some people doubted them. How else can we explain the testimonial poems by two of his former soldiers in eastern Europe, Ensign Thomas Carlton and Sergeant Edward Robinson? The poems appear in Smith's *Description of New England* (1616), though they seem almost out of place in a book concerning America. And their publication at the end of the book (1:362–62), evidently as an afterthought, rather than with the rest of the dedicatory poems (1:313–18), is quite surprising. Also, why would Smith register his official coat of arms, which recounted his exploits, in the office of the Herald of Arms on August 19, 1625 (3:129–30, 176–79), over twenty years after he had returned to England from eastern Europe? Both the 1616 testamentary poems and the 1625 recording served the same purpose: they proved to Smith's contemporaries that his incredible early adventures in eastern Europe occurred. The three duels in single combat were a glorious triumph. No English officer of Smith's time equaled it.[69] He was proud of that extraordinary feat and wanted it to be believed.

It is absurd to think that he would add a deliberate falsehood to the conclusion of a book featuring his amazing exploits as a young soldier in the Balkans. Obviously no one in 1630 doubted the story told in *The True Travels* that "*Pocahontas* saved his life" (3:237). If we had only this one statement that Pocahontas had saved his life, we would have an excellent reason to believe she did so—and no good reason to doubt it.

THREE

Considerations Bearing upon the Dispute

In addition to the overwhelming evidence that can be marshaled from Smith's eight reports that Pocahontas saved him, several other kinds of circumstantial evidence are pertinent to a consideration of the episode's possible validity.

Who Was Present?

The one white person there when Pocahontas supposedly saved Smith was Smith. He mentions by name only three Indians at the ceremony: Powhatan, Pocahontas, and the queen of Appamatuck. He also says, however, that "more then two hundred of those grim Courtiers stood wondering at him." He described their positions, with Powhatan seated "before a fire," with "a young wench of 16 or 18 yeares" on either side, "and along on each side the house, two rowes of men, and behind them as many women" (2:150). There can be no doubt that on this ceremonial occasion numerous Indians were present. We do not know if Pocahontas's sister Matachauna or her brother-in-law Uttamatomakkin or any of the other ten or so Indians who visited England with Pocahontas in 1616 were present on December 31, 1607, at the ceremony.[1]

Smith, however, was already well known to a number of Virginia Indians and became increasingly famous among the Indians the longer he stayed in Virginia. At the ceremony, he recognized the queen of Appamatuck, and she, of course, knew him from the first exploration of the James River, when the whites, returning down the James on May 26, 1607, stopped at her village.[2] Two additional Indians recognized him during his captivity with Opechancanough. One "called Kekataugh [Powhatan's brother], having received some kindnes of me at the Fort, kindly invited me to feast at his house" (1:51; mentioned only in *A True Relation*). Another, "Maocassater," seeing Smith suffer from the cold, "brought him his gowne, in requitall of some beads and toyes Smith had given him at his first arrivall in Virginia" (2:148; mentioned only in *The Generall Historie*). Certainly the Powhatan Indians he already knew, as well as those actually present when Pocahontas saved him, would have heard what happened to Smith during his captivity.

Long before Smith left Virginia in October 1609, possibly castrated by the explosion of his powder bag in his lap, which "tore the flesh from his body and thighes, nine or ten inches square in a most pittifull manner" (2:223), he had become famous among the Indians of the Chesapeake Bay area. In the spring of 1608 Powhatan designed a plan to get rid of the whites at Jamestown, but Smith threatened some offending Indians he took as captives with torture and learned Powhatan's plan from Macanoe, a Paspahegh councillor (1:89–93). Subsequently Powhatan called specifically for Smith's slaughter, but one after another, the Indian chiefs failed to kill him (even the far-off Patawomekes tried to carry out Powhatan's wishes [1:227; 2:166–67]). Powhatan himself testified in January 1608/9 that Smith had become a legend among the Indians, "and if a twig but breake, every one cryeth there commeth Captaine Smith" (2:196). After Powhatan himself failed to kill Smith, the overlord passed him on to the second greatest warrior, his brother Opechancanough, who had previously captured Smith. Opechancanough grandly failed when he attempted to ambush Smith and his men. He found himself challenged to single combat and then seized by the scalp lock and threatened in front of several hundred warriors (1:252; 1:432; 2:201–2).

Like all Powhatan's subchiefs, Opechancanough must have known the entire history of Smith's relations with the Indians in early Virginia, and he must have bitterly regretted that he turned Smith over to Powhatan and that Powhatan released Smith. Thousands of Powhatan Indians who knew of Smith must have heard of the Pocahontas episode by word of mouth. Though no one would have dared tell Powhatan that he made a terrible error when he freed the young white werowance, Powhatan himself recognized the mistake. Smith's Indian allies knew that Powhatan wanted to kill Smith and warned him. Long before Smith became famous in American history, most Indians of the western shore of the Chesapeake Bay had heard of the white leader and knew that Powhatan wanted him dead. Smith's activities were the stuff of legend among the Indians. When he returned from the first exploring expedition up the Chesapeake Bay, having encountered the Massawomecks (some group of the Six Nations), the Indians at Kecoughtan "would needs imagine we had bin at warres," so Smith told them he had fought with and vanquished this terrible enemy nation. "This rumor went faster up the river then our barge" (1:229).

On his second exploring trip up the bay, Smith fought with the Manahoacs (a Siouan people), the Massawomecks, and numerous other Indian tribes and met the Susquehanna Indians (2:175–78). All these battles and Smith's meeting with the dreaded Susquehannas would also have been reported, by rumor, at least, among the Powhatan Indians. In the spring of 1609, when Smith imprisoned two brothers and then released one to bring back a stolen pistol, the other seemingly suffocated in prison with excessive smoke. Smith, however, was able to bring him to consciousness "with aquavitae and vinegar." Thereafter it "was spread amongst all the Salvages for a miracle, that Captaine Smith could make a man alive that is dead" (1:262). After Smith left Virginia in the fall of 1609, the whites told the Indians he was dead. But the Indians did not believe it, and when Uttamatomakkin went to England seven years later, Powhatan commanded him to look for Smith there (2:261). Further, Purchas testified in 1613 that the Indians still spoke of Smith and asked about him.[3] Not until Nemattanow or Jack of the Feather appeared among the Powhatans did the Indians acquire another medicine man who inspired as much superstition and as many stories as did Smith (2:292).[4] It seems extremely unlikely that the Powhatan Indians would not have known that the great white warrior was one of their own, sponsored by Pocahontas and adopted into the tribe.

Past scholars, beginning with Deane and Adams, have remarked that only Smith was present when Pocahontas supposedly saved him. They discounted the Indians. But Powhatan, Pocahontas, the queen of Appamatuck, and "more than two hundred" other Indians were present. Surely Opechancanough, if he was not present when Smith was saved by Pocahontas, must have heard how and why the English werowance whom he had captured was released. Though Pocahontas died in 1616/17 and Powhatan died in 1618, many other Indians present when Pocahontas saved Smith on December 31, 1607, must have been still living in 1624. Numerous Indians knew the truth. We must conclude that many old Virginia hands who were living in England during the years that Smith was publishing his Virginia materials either knew or had the opportunity to know the details of his captivity.

The whites present in early Virginia could have, at least until the death of Opechancanough in 1644 and probably for some years thereafter, learned the truth of the Pocahontas episode from the Powhatan Indians. Every Indian expert and every white with many Indian contacts—that is, nearly every white person living in Virginia before 1622 and most whites living there before 1644—could have learned the truth from the Indians, and many probably did. Let me name some of the obvious persons. Among the first explorers, there was Captain John Martin (d. 1632?), George Percy (d. 1632), Nathaniel Powell (d. 1622?), and Anas Todkill (evidently in London in 1612). Unfortunately, Edward Maria Wingfield died about 1613, and Captain Christian Newport died about 1617. Among the Indian experts were Henry Spelman (d. 1623), Thomas Savage (d. c. 1632), William White (an original Jamestown colonist who returned to London), and Thomas Dale's man, who was present with Pocahontas in London in 1616. Among the persons in the first supply were Nathaniel Causey (d. post–1627), Michael and William Fettiplace (both in London in 1622), and David and Richard Wiffin (both in London in 1616). In the second supply, there were Thomas Abbay (in London in 1612), John Codrington (in London by 1616), Rawley Crashaw (in London by 1616), Richard Pots (back in London by 1612), and Francis West (d. 1633?). The later administrators included Captain Samuel Argall (who captured Pocahontas and later took her to

England, d. 1626), Ralph Hamor (d. 1626), and George Sandys (d. 1643/44). All these colonists, and others, spoke time and again to Indians who knew the truth of the Pocahontas story. If Smith had lied about the episode, numerous white persons could and would have learned that he had lied.

The Indian Ritual

One traditional reason for believing that Pocahontas saved Smith is that such a ritual of death, sponsorship, and rebirth is typical of adoption into an Indian tribe. In 1862 an anonymous reviewer of Charles Deane in the *Southern Literary Messenger* pointed out a parallel, citing a "report of the Committee on Indian Affairs, in the House of Representatives, of the Congress of the U.S., presented February 28th, 1843." The congressional report said that the "act of this Indian girl revives the recollection of . . . the rescue of Captain Smith by . . . Pocahontas."[5] The story of Milly, the daughter of Hillis Hadjo, a Seminole chief, appeared frequently in middle and late nineteenth-century books concerning American Indians.[6]

Jarvis Morse, who used the 1891 edition of Adams's essay without realizing that it had been revised twice since its original appearance, mistakenly said that Adams claimed such behavior was unknown among Indians.[7] Adams, in fact, had read the *Messenger* reviewer in 1867 and therefore knew that Indian maidens sometimes saved the lives of captives. What Adams actually wrote in a passage added in 1891 was that "the mode of execution there described [beating out the brains of a victim] was uncommon, if not unknown, among the Indians of the sea-coast."[8] Though Smith had said in *A Map of Virginia* that beating out the brains was one of the three Indian methods of capital punishment, Adams in 1867 implicitly denied that

Indians executed people in this manner, arguing that Smith's witnessing an Indian's being beaten into insensibility inspired the Pocahontas episode.[9] In 1891 he made the denial explicit, claiming that East Coast Indians rarely, if ever, executed people in this manner. Either Adams had begun by then to forget his reading of Smith and Virginia history or he never knew the Virginia sources well. Smith reported in *The Generall Historie* that when two traitorous Dutchmen learned that Lord De La Warr had arrived in Virginia, they asked Powhatan if they could return to the English, but the chief replied: "You that have betrayed Captaine Smith to mee, will certainly betray me to this great Lord for your peace: so caused him men to beat out their braines" (2:226). Purchas wrote in 1617 that Uttamatomakkin told him of executing an Indian, "his brains being knocked out," at the direction of Powhatan. Henry Spelman also reported that for robbing another Indian, an Indian thief "was knockt on the heade and being deade his lodge was burnt."[10]

Smith's advocates, from the *Messenger* reviewer to John Gould Fletcher, Bradford Smith, and Philip L. Barbour, all claimed that the Pocahontas episode fits in with what we know of Indian customs.[11] They made the further point that Smith could hardly have known that the Pocahontas episode would match the findings of later ethnologists. Smith himself thought that the Indians were fattening him up to make him a better sacrifice. But with the advantage of hindsight, it makes perfect sense that the Powhatans were adopting him into the tribe and that Pocahontas was his chosen sponsor. Smith's partisans said that if Smith made up the Pocahontas episode, then he had the incredible good fortune to create one that makes good sense three centuries later in light of what we now know concerning adoption into Indian tribes.[12]

But Smith no doubt read about a somewhat similar episode years before he published any references to Pocahontas's saving him. Juan Ortiz, a soldier with Pánfilo de Narváez in 1528, had been lured ashore near Tampa, Florida, and captured by Indians. They prepared to burn him to death, but he was saved by the daughter of Chief Ucita, who said "that one only Christian could do him neither hurt nor good" and "that it was more for his honour to keepe him as a captive."[13] Richard Hakluyt translated the tract from the Spanish and published it in 1609. Smith was living in London at the time. It is practically unthinkable that he would not have read a pamphlet entitled *Virginia Richly Valued*. So one could suppose, as the novelist James Branch Cabell has speculated, that Smith was inspired by the Ortiz story and made up the Pocahontas episode thereafter. To me Cabell's theory seems as farfetched as his earlier hypothesis that Smith created the episode in imitation of the Miranda-Ferdinand episode in Shakespeare's *Tempest*.[14] As Frances Mossiker has pointed out, numerous classical and medieval analogues are known. Mossiker also noted that the publication of the Ortiz story destroys the case for Smith's advocates who argued that what happened to him was fairly common among Indian captives but that he could not have known it at the time.[15] I agree. The argument is invalid.

The Special Relationship

Both Wyndham Robertson in 1860 and William Wirt Henry in 1875 called attention to the special relationship that existed between Smith and Pocahontas after his captivity. Henry argued, "There are several incidents related of Pocahontas which have never been questioned, and which cannot be well explained except upon the theory that she had done Smith some great service while he was a prisoner." He pointed out that *The Generall Historie* "relates numerous instances of Smith's great regard for her after his return from captivity" and that *A True Relation* "itself contains an incident which affords strong internal evidence of the truth of the subsequent statement of Smith as to his rescue." Henry then cited the passage near the end of *A True Relation* where Smith tells of Powhatan's sending Pocahontas, "his Daughter, a child of tenne yeares old, which not only for feature, countenance, and proportion, much exceedeth any of the rest of his people, but for wit, and spirit, the only Nonpariel of his Country" to secure the release of the Paspahegh prisoners that Smith had taken (1:93). Henry commented, "Why the crafty savage should have risked his own 'deerest daughter' at such a tender age on such an errand, is inexplicable, unless we are to believe that she had herself saved Smith's life before that time, and that it was well judged that Smith would not refuse her any request; and indeed he did give up the prisoners to her, after refusing them to others." Citing the same passage in 1860, Robertson questioned: Did not her intercession "seem to imply some peculiar and strong ground of claim on her part to his grateful recognition?" [16]

Without mentioning Robertson, whom he may not have read, or Henry, whom he obviously did read, Adams attempted to reply to the special relationship argument in the 1891 revision of his essay. He added several paragraphs dealing with Pocahontas in Smith's *True Relation*. First, he maintained that *A True Relation* had "every appearance of telling the whole share she had in Smith's affairs." [17] But of course *A True Relation* was written and published in 1608, before Pocahontas came late one night in January 1608/9 to warn Smith of Powhatan's plan (1:274; 2:198). Second, he quoted the passage cited by Robertson and Henry and argued: "Had Pocahontas saved Smith's

life four months before, Smith would have been likely to surrender the prisoners out of gratitude to her, rather than 'in
regard of her father's kindnesse in sending' his favorite child
to ask a return for his own hospitality."[18] That quibble was the
best he could do.

Though Adams had the last word regarding Pocahontas as
intercessor for the Paspaheghs, his reasoning in part seems to
me to smack of the anachronistic, "scientific" school rather
than the "reckless, hit or miss" style characteristic of the Elizabethan and Jacobean periods that Thoreau so greatly admired.
Moreover, by 1891 Adams had evidently forgotten that the very
reason he said should have been in Smith's *True Relation* was
present in *The Proceedings*. In one section, the author, presumably Anas Todkill, wrote that Smith delivered the Paspahegh
prisoners to Pocahontas, "for whose sake only he fained to save
their lives and graunt them liberty" (1:221).

As we have seen, Henry Adams said that if he had read the
review of Deane's edition of Wingfield in the *Southern Literary
Messenger* of November–December 1862, he would not have
changed anything he wrote, but he might have added a paragraph or two. He did so when he first revised his piece in 1871.
The *Messenger* author had cited Smith's story of Pocahontas's
warning him (and perhaps saving his life) and eighteen companions in late January 1608/9, as told in *The Generall Historie*.
Invited by Powhatan, Smith went to Werowocomoco, where
Powhatan and he enacted the last of their ritualistic dances of
death, with the subtle Smith attempting to bargain for corn
and other food, while the wily Powhatan constantly tried to
get the whites into a defenseless posture in order to slaughter
them. The last night at Werowocomoco, Pocahontas came to
warn Smith that Powhatan was lying in wait to kill him and
his companions while they ate. The *Messenger* author wrote,

"Smith would have rewarded her with such toys as she was fond of, but with tears streaming down her cheeks, she said, that she would not dare to be seen to have them, for if her father should know it she would die, and so she ran away by herself as she had come."[19]

In his 1871 revision, Adams pointed out that *A Map of Virginia* "not only mentions Pocahontas, but introduces her as the savior of Smith's life, although it says no word of her most famous act in this character."[20] Adams added:

> The assumed writer [of this part of *The Proceedings*] took occasion to defend Smith against certain charges, one of them being an alleged scheme on his part of marrying Powhatan's daughter Pocahontas in order to acquire a claim to the throne. The writer denied the charge, and added:—
>
> "It is true she was the very nonparell of his kingdome, and at most not past 13 or 14 yeares of age. Very often shee came to our fort with what shee could get for Captaine Smith, that ever loved and used all the countrie well, but her especially he ever much respected; and she so well requited it that when her father intended to have surprised him, shee, by stealth in the darke night, came through wild woods and told him of it."[21]

Adams then continued with his previous argument that "this Oxford tract of 1612 may be considered as decisive of the fact that, down to that date, the story of Pocahontas had not been made public."[22] But the quotation does not disprove the special relationship theory (indeed, it strengthens it), nor does it mean that the author of this part of *The Proceedings*, presumably William Fettiplace, did not know of the earlier Pocahontas episode.[23] Adams again anachronistically assumed that the Smith-Pocahontas episode had extraordinary importance before poets and other writers made it famous. Furthermore, common sense tells us that if the writer was with Smith at Werowocomoco—and the account makes it clear that he was—then Pocahontas's saving the writer's, Smith's, and the entire party's lives would have been, to the writer, the most important and dramatic proof of her regard for Smith. Furthermore, the author had no good reason to mention Pocahontas's earlier saving of Smith.

Other evidences of a special relationship between Pocahontas and Smith exist that Robertson, the *Messenger* reviewer, and Henry ignore. After Smith's return from captivity to Jamestown in January 1607/8, the Powhatan confederacy began supplying the colonists with corn products and deer, "each weeke once or twice" (1:61). "This relief," Smith wrote to Queen Anne in 1616, "was commonly brought us by this Lady Pocahontas" (2:259). Retelling the story in *The Generall Historie*, Smith said that "now ever once in foure or five dayes, Pocahontas with her attendants, brought him so much provision, that saved many of their lives, that els for all this had starved with hunger" (2:152). Evidently the Indians had abundant food from the previous harvest until sometime in April. But in May, after bad relations developed and the Indians stole tools, shot at the whites, and attempted to seize the fort, the colonists captured and jailed several Paspaheghs. Then followed the incident that Robertson and Henry cite from *A True Relation* and that Adams tried to refute in 1891, though he had forgotten the version in *The Proceedings*.

In October 1608, when Smith and only four comrades visited Werowocomoco and thought the Indians were planning to attack them, Pocahontas appeared to assure Smith that the surprising noise and appearance of the Indians was only an entertainment, "A Virginia Maske," by the Indian maidens in their honor (2:182–83). Smith saw her only one more time in Virginia, when Pocahontas came to warn him of Powhatan's plan to kill him as he was leaving Werowocomoco.

Pocahontas did two other special favors for the English, however. Before Smith left Werowocomoco for Opechanca-nough's residence at Pamunkey, a tragedy occurred at James-town. Matthew Scrivener, whom Smith had left in charge, was drowned in the James River with Captain Richard Waldo, Anthony Gosnold, and eight others. Richard Wiffin came to let Smith know. By the time Wiffin arrived at Werowoco-moco, Smith had left. Powhatan ordered that Wiffin be killed, but as Robertson noted, Pocahontas hid him and said he had gone off in another direction. So Wiffin, who later joined the Fettiplaces in writing a testimonial poem for Smith (1:317–18; 2:229–30), was able to journey on to Pamunkey with the news. After Smith left Virginia in October 1609, Pocahontas performed another favor for the English, as both Robertson and the *Messenger* reviewer noted.[24] When Powhatan wiped out John Ratcliffe and thirty other men who were attempting to trade in December 1609, Pocahontas saved the youth Henry Spelman (2:232). Smith added this detail to *The Generall Histo-rie*, but it was not in *The Proceedings* (cf. 1:275). After all, Smith said he wrote *The Generall Historie* to memorialize the names of the adventurers who partook in the action. Smith obviously thought that action of Pocahontas in saving Spelman deserved to be remembered.[25] After citing the Spelman story, the *Mes-senger* reviewer sarcastically asked Charles Deane, "Is this also another 'marvellous story,' an additional embellishment?"[26]

Smith saw Pocahontas one last time, in the fall of 1616, at Brentford, England. Pocahontas was there with her husband, John Rolfe, and "divers" of Smith's friends. Smith told the story in *The Generall Historie*, immediately after printing his letter to Queen Anne concerning Pocahontas. In the letter, he had said that Pocahontas was "of so great a spirit, how ever her stature" (2:260). Her behavior proved his judgment: "After a modest salutation, without any word, she turned about, obscured her face, as not seeming well contented; and in that humour her husband, with divers others, we all left her two or three houres, repenting my selfe to have writ she could speake English. But not long after, she began to talke, and remembred mee well what courtesies shee had done: saying, You did promise Powhatan what was yours should bee his, and he the like to you; you called him father being in his land a stranger, and by the same reason so must I doe you" (2:261).

But in tradition-bound England, Smith thought it would be a mistake for Pocahontas, "because she was a Kings daughter," to call him father, and so he tried to explain to her that she should not. But Pocahontas was already angry with Smith for not coming to see her earlier, and his answer further aroused her. She actually accused the old soldier of moral cowardice: "With a well set countenance she said, Were you not afraid to come into my fathers Countrie, and caused feare in him and all his people (but mee) and feare you here I should call you father; I tell you then I will, and you shall call mee childe, and so I will bee for ever and ever your Countrieman. They did tell us alwaies you were dead, and I knew no other till I came to Plimoth; yet Powhatan did command Uttamatomakkin to seeke you, and know the truth, because your Countriemen will lie much" (2:261).

The interview with Pocahontas, like the letter to Queen Anne and Smith's concluding remarks on her (2:261–62), confirms that a special relationship existed between Smith and Pocahontas. Though Henry Adams did his best to discredit the special relationship argument after it was introduced by Smith's Southern defenders, Adams himself had earlier been convinced and had written Palfrey in 1861 that the relationship proved Pocahontas had saved Smith:

> In Virginia it seems also to have been known from the first, for we are told from other colonists that the same Pocahontas continued to have a great affection for Smith and the English, and not only saved them from starvation but brought them information at the risk of her life. What her motive was I cannot understand, for she was a mere child, only twelve years old, and could hardly have had a sentimental attachment to Smith; yet her services ceased when he left the province; and she went off to live with a relation on the Potomac. Perhaps it was some wild-Indian semi-lunacy that drove her to it, for I confess I am very skeptical about any pure philanthropy in an Indian child that would drive her through a forest in mid-winter many miles in order to betray her father. Such an act implies strong motives.[27]

But Adams suppressed his doubts when he wrote his essay.

The best logical explanation for the special relationship that existed between Smith and Pocahontas from the time of his captivity throughout the rest of her life is that she saved him during his captivity. Frances Mossiker gives the special relationship theory as a principal reason for her belief that Pocahontas saved Smith.[28] Pocahontas's saving Henry Spelman after the departure of Smith, however, may suggest that she was simply a humane person. Nevertheless, Smith, Pocahontas, and their contemporaries all behaved as if a special relationship existed between the two. I believe such a relationship did exist.

Evidence from Purchas

The Reverend Samuel Purchas (1577–1626), who succeeded Richard Hakluyt as the greatest collector of accounts of English voyages, was an authority on English overseas expansion. He met Smith before 1612. From 1613 to 1625 Purchas published accounts of Virginia within the successive editions of his gazetteer. Living in London, Samuel Purchas knew many leaders of the Virginia Company, he corresponded with colonists in Virginia, he collected manuscripts concerning Virginia, and he interviewed Virginia colonists who returned to London. Purchas came to know Smith well. After Purchas's death in 1626, Smith testified that he was a "Gentleman whose person I loved, and whose memory and vertues I will ever honour" (3:96).

The best evidence for Smith's contemporaneous reputation is to be gained from the popular gazetteer that Purchas published in 1613, 1614, 1617, and 1625. Purchas obviously accepted the Smith-Pocahontas story as true, for he reprinted it in 1625. He had conducted an extensive series of interviews in 1616/17 with Pocahontas, John Rolfe, Uttamatomakkin and his wife, Matachauna, and other Indians and Indian authorities, including the interpreter, "Sir Thomas Dale's man," Samuel Argall, and Thomas Dale. As we will see, Henry Adams misrepresented Purchas in an attempt to discredit Smith. Other historians, from George Bancroft to William Wirt Henry and beyond, have used Purchas to validate Smith.

Purchas borrowed Smith's manuscripts and used them in the first edition of his great gazetteer, *Purchas His Pilgrimage; or, Relations of the World and the Religions in All Ages and Places Discovered* (1613). Entered in the Stationers' Register on August 7, 1612, the work was essentially completed before then, though "The Epistle Dedicatorie" is dated November 5, 1612. Purchas talked with Smith about Virginia and the Indians there and quoted details of conversations with him.[29] Purchas obviously believed and respected Smith and told the story of Virginia's early years from Smith's point of view. Thus, after telling of the early dissensions among the leaders of the Virginia Colony,

Purchas wrote: "A cleare skie did afterwards appeare in their agreement on the choise of Captaine *Smith* for their President, who hauing before fallen into the hands of the Virginians, had beene presented Prisoner to *Powhatan*, where hee tooke aduantage by that disaduantage, to acquaint himselfe with the State and condition of the Countrie and Inhabitants."[30]

In the 1613 *Pilgrimage*, Purchas gave as the main reason for Smith's return to England the "hurt by gunne-powder . . . which forced him for his recouerie to set sayle for England." He quoted Smith in conversation as saying that he had been "in many places of Asia and Europe, in some of Africa and America, but of all, holds Virginia by the naturall endowments, the fittest place for an earthly Paradise." Purchas also testified that the Indians held Smith in high regard, and "still as I haue been told by some that haue since beene there, they doe affect him, and will ask of him." Of course Purchas talked with other persons concerning Virginia, as well as with the Virginia Company officials in London. He quoted Henry Spelman and mentioned conversations with Samuel Argall.[31]

The 1613 *Pilgrimage* was a success, and Purchas followed it with a second edition, revised and expanded, in 1614. Purchas again especially praised Smith — "by the industry of *Smith*, *James Town* was builded" — though he knew Edward Maria Wingfield's manuscript of the early events at Jamestown and referred to conversations with Wingfield. He cited a letter and a "book" by the Reverend Alexander Whitaker in Virginia and mentioned conversations with Samuel Argall on the "health and welfare of the Colonie." Purchas quoted a manuscript by George Percy and paraphrased conversations with William White, who had lived with the Indians and who evidently returned to England with Percy in July 1612. In the 1614 *Pilgrimage*, Purchas mentioned Pocahontas for the first time:

"They tooke *Pokahuntis* (*Powhatans* deerest daughter) prisoner, and for her ransome had Corne, and redliuerie of their Prisoners and Weapons." [32]

The third edition of the *Pilgrimage*, again revised and enlarged, appeared in 1617. Purchas corrected his former notice of Pocahontas, who had not been ransomed but was held by the whites until she fell in love with John Rolfe and married him. In 1616 she and Rolfe visited England, where Purchas met her and the other Indians who came with her. Purchas now wrote: "They tooke *Pokohuntis* (*Powhatans* dearest daughter) prisoner, a matter of good consequence to them, of best to her, by this meanes being become a Christian, & married to Master *Rolph*, an English Gentleman." Purchas attached a marginal note: "Her true Name was *Matokes*, which they concealed from the English, in a superstitious feare of hurt by the English if her name were knowne: she is now Christened *Rebecca*." The 1617 *Pilgrimage* added several details to Purchas's account of Virginia that he had learned from conversations with Rolfe, Percy, and Wingfield. [33]

The group that came to England with Sir Thomas Dale in 1616 greatly interested Purchas. Besides Rolfe and other whites, Pocahontas, Uttamatomakkin and his wife, Matachauna, and more than ten additional Indians were present and available to provide information. Rolfe set Purchas straight about the purpose of a huskanawing ceremony that Smith and White had described and loaned him a copy of a manuscript he had written, "The True Relation of the State of Virginia," which Purchas used to good purpose. Although Purchas cited various conversations with Virginia authorities, including John Rolfe and Thomas Dale, his main 1617 Virginia additions came from Uttamatomakkin. Purchas identified him as "an experienced Man and Counseller to *Opochancanough*," married to "*Mata-*

chauna one of *Powhatans* daughters." Purchas quoted Uttama-tomakkin extensively on the Indians' "opinions and ceremonies in Religion." [34]

In his last work and his masterpiece, *Hakluytus Posthumus; or, Purchas His Pilgrimes* (1625), Purchas expanded his Virginia materials, adding sources from published tracts by Smith and others and also using additional manuscript materials. From *The Generall Historie* he reprinted the story of Pocahontas's saving Smith. He added details to what he had said in 1617 about Uttamatomakkin: "With this savage I have often conversed at my good friends Master Doctor Goldstone, where he was a frequent guest; and where I have both seen him sing and dance his diabolicall measures, and heard him discourse of his Countrey and Religion, Sir Tho. Dales man being the Interpretour." [35] Purchas wrote about Pocahontas:

> And his [Rolfe's] wife did not onely accustome her selfe to civilitie, but still carried her selfe as the Daughter of a King, and was accordingly respected, not onely by the Company, which allowed provision for her selfe and her sonne, but of divers particular persons of Honor, in their hopefull zeale by her to advance Christianitie. I was present, when my Honorable & Reverend Patron the L. Bishop of London, Doctor King entertained her with festivall state and pompe, beyond what I have seene in his great hospitalitie afforded to other Ladies. [36]

Purchas concluded his 1625 account of Pocahontas with her supposedly Christian bearing at death.

Henry Adams tried to counter the possible use of Purchas as a witness to Smith's reliability. Following Deane, Adams pointed out that Samuel Purchas had met Pocahontas in 1616, that he had often talked with Uttamatomakkin "at my good friend's Master Doctor Goldstone, where he was a frequent

guest," and that he knew John Rolfe, "who lent him his manuscript discourse on Virginia." Adams also quoted Purchas saying that "he was present when my Honorable and Reverend
Patron the Lord Bishop of London, Dr. King, entertained her
with festivall state and pompe beyond what I have seen in
his great hospitalitee afforded to other ladies." [37] Adams said
that the "edition of 1617," the third edition of *Purchas His
Pilgrimage,*

> reflects the interest which was then so generally felt in the his-
> tory of Rebecca Rolfe; and we may expect, with almost absolute
> certainty, to find in it all the new information that could be col-
> lected in regard to her life. Yet here, again, no allusion can be
> found to her heroic intervention on behalf of Smith, the story
> of whose captivity is simply copied from Symond's quarto of
> 1612 [i.e., *The Proceedings*]; and the diffuse comments on men
> and manners in Virginia contain no trace of what would have
> been correctly regarded as the most extraordinary incident in
> the colonial history.[38]

But the Virginia materials that Adams cited, ostensibly from
the third edition of *Purchas His Pilgrimage,* are actually from
the 1625 *Hakluytus Posthumus.*[39] As we have just seen, the 1617
edition contained only one sentence and one marginal note regarding Pocahontas. Information from Uttamatomakkin concerning the religion of the Indians and passages from Rolfe's
manuscript were far more interesting to Purchas. Despite, according to Adams, the supposed "timeliness" of information
concerning Pocahontas, Purchas pretty much ignored her in
1617. The references that Adams cited to Uttamatomakkin,
Dr. Goldstone, John Rolfe, Dr. King, and Pocahontas are all
actually from Purchas's *Hakluytus Posthumus.*[40] Adams implied
that Purchas added all these materials concerning Pocahon-

tas in the 1617 edition of his gazetteer. Adams's point was that since Purchas added so much new information concerning Pocahontas in 1617, he surely would have also added a reference to Pocahontas's saving Smith if she had actually saved him. So this additional material, supposedly in the 1617 edition, tended to prove that the Pocahontas story was unknown at the time. But since Purchas in fact added practically no new information concerning Pocahontas to the 1617 edition, why would he have added the information that Pocahontas saved Smith? At best, we must think that Adams was simply careless about the source of his quotation from Purchas.

Nor does Adams admit that the Pocahontas episode is, in fact, present in *Hakluytus Posthumus*, the actual source of his quotations. In his original 1867 essay, Henry Adams attacked George Bancroft for saying in the pre-1860 editions of his *History* that *A True Relation* "fully contained" the substance of the Pocahontas story. He also quoted Bancroft's revised note, in the post-1860 editions, that cited Deane's edition of Wingfield but disagreed with Deane's judgment on the validity of the Pocahontas incident. Bancroft had cited the three references to the Pocahontas incident that Deane dealt with and, in addition, noted, "In 1625, Purchas, who had many manuscripts on Virginia, gives the narrative a place in his Pilgrimes, as unquestionably authentic." [41] When he revised his essay again in 1891, Adams deleted Deane's post-1860 note. The 1862 anonymous essayist, whose review Deane sent Adams in 1867, had also pointed out that Purchas reprinted the Smith-Pocahontas story in 1625. [42] I must conclude that Adams either carelessly or deliberately misinformed his readers concerning what Purchas wrote in 1617 and that he knew but deliberately suppressed what Purchas published in 1625. [43]

William Wirt Henry did not attack Henry Adams for his

misinformation; perhaps Henry did not have access to the 1617 *Purchas His Pilgrimage*. He did, however, have a copy of *Hakluytus Posthumus*. Henry pointed out that Purchas stated he used manuscripts on Virginia by Rolfe and Smith. Purchas, he said, "tells us he had been thrown with Pocahontas while she was in England, and had frequently conversed with Rolfe and the Indian councillor, her brother-in-law who accompanied her." Like the *Messenger* reviewer, Henry pointed out that Purchas reprinted Smith's account of his being saved by Pocahontas. Henry argued: "With such opportunities of obtaining correct information on the matter in controversy, and with the high character borne by Purchas, his testimony may well be looked to as decisive of the question." [44]

I agree with William Wirt Henry that we could hardly have a better testimonial to the truth of the Pocahontas episode.[45] Purchas was in continued contact with the old Virginia hands, the Virginia Company authorities, and the court circle from before 1612 until his death in 1626. If Smith had lied about Pocahontas's saving him, Purchas would have heard from numerous people that he had lied, and Purchas would certainly have cast doubt upon the episode. Instead, he reprinted it. To believe that Smith lied about the Pocahontas episode, one must also believe that Purchas conspired in the lie with him.

Evidence from Old Virginia Hands

Charles Deane and Henry Adams found it incredible that the other authors of early Virginia accounts would have been silent about the Pocahontas episode if it had actually happened. They believed that Edward Maria Wingfield (who was present in Virginia while Smith was a captive), William Strachey, or Ralph Hamor would have mentioned it. But William Wirt

Henry quite rightly dismissed the argument. Wingfield dealt summarily with Smith's captivity in less than one hundred words and gave no details. Strachey and Hamor arrived after Smith had left Virginia. Strachey mentioned the captivity twice, but only to provide information that Smith learned about the customs and religion of the Indians during his captivity.[46] And Hamor said nothing about the events that took place before his arrival in Virginia. Wingfield, Strachey, and Hamor could not foresee that over two centuries later the Pocahontas incident would become the most famous episode in early Virginia history and that they themselves would be forgotten by all but scholars. Indeed, if someone had known and told them the anachronistic truth, they would have laughed at the absurdity of the idea. No one in Smith's day thought the Pocahontas episode especially important to Smith's reputation. Only the nineteenth-century poets, playwrights, novelists, and historians made it so.[47]

The *Messenger* author, reviewing Deane in 1862, pointed out that Smith "was often the subject of envy and detraction in his own day, yet his integrity was fully endorsed by his contemporaries," quoting as proof excerpts from the testamentary verses. William Wirt Henry argued that the Virginia Company evidently accepted the general truthfulness of *The Generall Historie* and that many individuals of the company must have known the truth. He quoted from the testamentary verses of Michael and William Fettiplace, John Codrington, Rawley Crashaw, and Samuel Purchas—all of whom praised Smith for veracity.[48] Henry evidently did not realize that all the verses he chose to cite except that by Samuel Purchas were reprinted from *A Description of New England* (1616), a work that appeared before any of Smith's published references to the Pocahontas episode.

Though I concluded the first section of this chapter with several categories of Virginians who surely had numerous occasions to learn the truth from the Indians, let me survey here those Virginia companions who wrote portions of *The Proceedings* and who evidently returned to England. They include Thomas Abbay (*CW* 1:135, 199), William Fettiplace (1:199, 258, 275), Richard Pots (1:199, 275), Nathaniel Powell (1:199, 233), Anas Todkill (1:221, 229, 233, 258), and David and Richard Wiffin (1:199, 258). Others, like Sir Samuel Argall (1580–1626), who abducted Pocahontas and wrote about her, must have known the truth of the Smith-Pocahontas episode; certainly Argall never denied its truth. Most of the following Virginia colonists returned to England and were probably living after the appearance of *The Generall Historie* in 1624: Nathaniel Causey (fl. 1608–27), who arrived in Virginia with Newport on the day that Smith returned from captivity, January 2, 1607/8, and returned to England in 1627 (3:125); John Codrington (1580s?–1622?), author of prefatory verses for *A Description of New England*, who was studying in the Inner Temple in 1616 when Dale arrived with Pocahontas, Rolfe, and other Indians (1:313); Rawley Crashaw, who came to Virginia with the second supply in 1608 and wrote prefatory verses for *A Description of New England* (1:316); Michael and William Fettiplace (fl. 1608–22), joint authors (with Richard Wiffin) of prefatory verses for *A Description of New England*, whom Smith called upon in 1622 as witnesses to his treatment of Opechancanough (1:317–18); Ralph Hamor (fl. 1609–26), author of *A True Discourse of the Present Estate of Virginia* (1615) who had no reason to mention this story but was nevertheless in a position to deny it if it were not true; John Rolfe (1585–1622), husband of Pocahontas; Thomas Savage (1594?–post 1631), Indian expert who came with the first supply in 1608; David and Richard Wiffin, who came with the first supply in 1608 and wrote commendatory verses in 1616 (1:317–18); and Sir George Yeardley (1588–1627), later governor, who sailed for Virginia in 1609.[49]

Most of these old Virginia hands were still alive in 1622 and 1624 when Smith published his comments on Pocahontas. As William Wirt Henry pointed out, Smith even specifically called upon George Percy, Francis West, and the Fettiplaces in 1622, all of whom were then in London, to testify that he had successfully subdued Opechancanough. Samuel Purchas and numerous members of the Virginia Company must have known most of these Virginia colonists. If one is to believe that Smith lied about being saved by Pocahontas, then one must believe that the old Virginia hands conspired with Smith in the lie. To think that Smith's friends might have joined him in a conspiracy to lie about the Pocahontas episode might make sense to some South-baiters, but as the *Messenger* reviewer, Wyndham Robertson, and William Wirt Henry have all pointed out, at least a few old Virginia hands actively disliked Smith. Henry stated: "Smith had bitter enemies who would have been glad to have exposed him had it been in their power."[50] If Smith had lied about the Pocahontas episode, these old Virginia hands surely would have called him a liar.

The defenders of Smith have generally, however, not identified Smith's enemies or given the reasons for knowing that they were his enemies. Edward Maria Wingfield (fl. 1586–post–1612) charged Smith with mutiny on the voyage to Virginia. After being elected president of the first council, Wingfield made a speech explaining why Smith, contrary to instructions, should not serve on the council. Wingfield was deposed by Smith and the other members of the council on September 10, 1607. He was brought to trial for charging Smith with mutiny and for other libels, found guilty, and fined two hundred pounds. In 1608, back in England, Wingfield wrote a discourse defending himself and his actions as president. He recorded that on September 11, 1607, Smith testified against him: "Then start vp Master Smyth, and said that I had tould him playnly how he lied, and that I said though wee were equall heere [in Virginia], yet if he [Smith] were in England he [Wingfield] would thinck scorne his man [Wingfield's servant] should be my [Smith's] Companyon." Wingfield despised Smith. As I have shown, Wingfield talked with Purchas, but Wingfield's death date is unknown. He probably died before 1624, when the Pocahontas story received major publicity.[51]

Captain John Martin (c. 1567–1632?), another original colonist and member of the first Virginia Council, was repeatedly satirized by Smith in *A True Relation* and in all of Smith's later publications on Virginia. Anas Todkill, Martin's servant who became one of Smith's most trusted companions, mocked Martin's timorousness in *The Proceedings*, and the editor or printer even called attention to Martin's pusillanimous behavior with a marginal heading, "The adventures of Captain Martin" (1:221; cf. 2:158, 160). Purchas reprinted *The Proceedings* and its sarcastic marginal heading in *Hakluytus Posthumus*.[52] Smith sent Martin back to England in disgrace in 1608, but Martin returned in 1609 and was evidently one of those who trumped up charges against Smith after Percy was elected president of the council on September 10, 1609.[53] Certainly Martin, who occasionally visited England and who lived on in Virginia after Smith's death, would have seized the chance to discredit Smith. Martin did not attempt to do so.

George Percy and Francis West, whom Smith specifically called upon in 1622 as witnesses to the way he treated Opechancanough, were both enemies. On the very page that he cited Percy and West, he mentioned the Pocahontas incident for the first time in print. George Percy (1580–1632), younger brother of Henry Percy, ninth earl of Northumberland, sailed with the original colonists in 1607. He presided over the colony during the "starving time" after Smith left. The account in *The Proceedings* says, "Now wee all found the want of Captaine *Smith*, yea his greatest maligners could then curse his losse" (1:275). Such was, according to Smith and his partisans, the colony under Percy's leadership.[54]

Percy stayed on in Virginia until April 1612. Percy's family home, Syon House, in Middlesex, was just across the river from Brentford, where Smith went to see Pocahontas, Rolfe, and "divers" of his other old Virginia acquaintances in 1616. Percy too must have seen this group during the time they were in England. Percy was in England in 1622 when Smith published *New Englands Trials*. He evidently remained in England until 1625. Probably in 1624 or 1625, he wrote "A Trewe Relacyon of the Procedeinges and Ocurrentes of Momente wch have Hapned in Virginia." He was clearly angry about his portrayal in Smith's writings and evidently wrote his essay in reply to the appearance of *The Generall Historie* in 1624, where, of course, the Pocahontas episode is fully told. In his "Trewe Relacyon," Percy called Smith "an Ambityous unworthy and vayneglorious fellowe attempteing to take all Mens Authoreties from them," but he did not call him a liar and did not question the veracity of the Pocahontas episode.[55] Surely if Pocahontas had not saved Smith, Percy would have known about it and would have refuted the story. But Percy was silent in his "Trewe Relacyon" and afterward about the incident.

The other enemy called upon in 1622 to testify to the truth of Smith's treatment of Opechancanough was Captain Francis West (1586–1633?), who came to Virginia with the second supply in 1608. A younger brother of Lord De La Warr, West stayed on in Virginia, making various trips back to England, and served as governor in 1628–29. After the arrival of the remnants of the Somer-Gates supply in August 1609, West was among those who called Smith's authority into question. With 120 men, West went to settle at "The Falls" but chose a flood plain by the James River for the settlement. Smith thought the place impractical and bought from Powhatan the settlement called Powhatan on high ground not far from the James. But West and his companions refused to settle there, "contemning both him, his kinde care and authoritie" (2:221). According to the confused and malicious youth Henry Spelman, West quarreled with and insulted Smith, who "at the time repliede litell but afterward comspired with the Powhatan to kill Capt. weste." West was in England in 1622, disliked Smith, and had continued connections with Virginia until after Smith's death.[56] If he could have caused Smith trouble or proven him to be a liar, West would have done so.

Numerous old Virginia hands lived on in England and in Virginia after the Pocahontas episode appeared in print in 1622 and 1624. Charles Deane and Henry Adams thought it strange that none of them, particularly the writers, described or referred to the story. But as I have argued, there was no reason for them to do so if Pocahontas had actually saved Smith, for the episode had not in the early seventeenth century achieved the mythic dimensions with which the nineteenth century imbued it. One might as easily ask why they didn't refer to the time that Smith was tied to a tree and the Indians, after Opechancanough held up the compass, decided not to shoot him. In fact, the Pocahontas episode was not especially important to Smith's contemporaries. But if the story had been false, it would have been amazing indeed if Smith's contemporaries — friends as well as foes — had not denied the story. Contrary to the reasoning of Deane and Adams, the silence of the old Virginia hands proves that Pocahontas saved Smith.

Evidence from Contemporaries

Besides the former Virginia colonists and Samuel Purchas, several groups of people should have known the truth of the Pocahontas episode.

The Council of the Virginia Company

The London Virginia Company Council met frequently, heard all the major news from Virginia, and publicized the colony.[57] The early treasurer and chief executive officer of the council was Sir Thomas Smith. The treasurer's chief assistant or deputy was Robert Johnson, a London alderman, who wrote much of the early official propaganda for the company.[58] In 1619 Sir Edwin Sandys, who was knighted at the Charterhouse on May 11, 1603, along with Sir Robert Bruce Cotton and others, became the treasurer.[59] John Ferrar became the deputy. All the very active members of the Virginia Company read numerous manuscript reports and all the published materials, and they continually interviewed those who returned from Virginia. The surviving records of John Smyth of Nibley testify to the close attention that council members paid to the company.[60] A continuous record of the Virginia Company Council meetings exists from April 28, 1619, to June 7, 1624.[61] In the first year the council held nineteen meetings. Only the attendance of the gentlemen was carefully recorded, "with others" being a common notation at the end of the list of those present. Members who attended 10 or more meetings were

Henry Wriothesley, earl of Southampton (attended 13 meetings), William Cavendish, duke of Newcastle (14), William, Baron Paget (13), Sir John Danvers (14), Sir Edwin Sandys (12), Mr. Richard Berblock (13), Mr. Arthur Bromfield (13), Mr. Richard Caswell (11), Mr. Francis Covell (11), Mr. John Ferrar (15), Mr. Thomas Gibbs (12), Mr. Edmond Hacket (12), Mr. John Smyth of Nibley (12), and Mr. George Swinhowe (12). At least these fourteen persons attended most meetings during that year and made decisions on every aspect of Virginia life. They had funds invested and heard news of all important Virginia events. Furthermore, the period 1619 to 1620 was after the heyday of the Virginia Company. The Virginia Company Council of a decade before, 1609–10, was probably more active, with more meetings and better attendance.

The Virginia Company Council must have interviewed Captain John Smith when he returned from Virginia in late 1609, just as they did other Virginia hands in later years. They must also have met Pocahontas, John Rolfe, Uttamatomakkin and his wife, Matachauna, and other Virginians, including Thomas Dale's interpreter, in 1616. We know that during Pocahontas's visit, the council voted her an allowance of four pounds a week and evidently appointed Dr. Theodore Goulston, a council member, to be in charge of her entertainment.[62]

If Smith lied about the Pocahontas episode in his letter to the queen of 1616 or in his publications of 1622 and 1624, the Virginia Company Council would have known it. Smith had fallen out with the company and had become identified with its rivals long before 1616.[63] The council members would have been glad to have exposed Smith if they had known he lied. Evidently none of the returning Virginia hands, including Samuel Argall and Thomas Dale, ever hinted that Smith lied. The members of the Virginia Company Council, the London experts on Virginia, never heard anything that suggested Smith fabricated the Pocahontas episode.

Royal Commissioners

The royal commissioners who spent at least six weeks hearing testimony in May and early June 1623 were another group of disinterested administrators who heard the Pocahontas story and who interviewed all the old Virginia hands and all the Virginia Company officials. A list of the commissioners, in the chronological order of their knighthood, follows: Sir William Jones (1566–1640), chairman, was knighted at Whitehall on March 12, 1616/17. Jones, who is listed in the *Dictionary of National Biography*, was judge of the king's bench from 1624 to 1640.[64] Sir Henry Spiller was knighted at Whitehall on July 20, 1618. Rumors of his impending promotion to chancellor of the exchequer occur repeatedly in John Chamberlain's letters.[65] Sir Nicholas Fortescue the elder (1575?–1633) was a Roman Catholic who became chamberlain of the exchequer in 1618. In 1610 he was appointed commissioner of James's household and of the navy. He was knighted at Whitehall on February 2, 1618/19.[66] The *DNB* reports that "during 1622 and 1623 his name appears as serving on royal commissions, to inquire into the state of the plantations of Virginia and of Ireland."[67]

Three other members of the Jones commission were knighted at Whitehall along with Fortescue on February 2, 1618/19: Sir Francis Gofton, auditor of the exechequer; Sir William Pitt; and Sir Richard Sutton, also auditor of the exechequer. According to John Chamberlain, these knights were "employed about the matters of the houshold and navie."[68]

The most recent knight was Sir Henry Bourchier, knighted at Theobald's on November 4, 1621.[69]

Smith mentioned the Pocahontas story in his sworn testimony before the commissioners. If it had been false, this group of loyal administrators would have heard from other attesters that Smith lied. What possible reason could he have had for lying in such a situation?

Dedicatees of Smith's Books

The nobles to whom Smith dedicated his books would not have allowed him to use their names if he were thought to be a liar. It would have brought them shame. Since the only question in dispute is the Pocahontas episode, I will consider only those books published in and after 1622, when Smith first said that "God made Pocahontas the Kings daughter the means to deliver me" (1:432) in the revised edition of *New Englands Trials*. That book, like *A Description of New England* (1616), was dedicated to Prince Charles (1:421). As I pointed out above, Smith probably presented his letter to Queen Anne when Prince Charles received him in 1616 and changed a number of Indian place-names in New England to English ones. It would have been an outrageous insult to Prince Charles for Smith to have lied in *New Englands Trials*.

The dedicatee of *The Generall Historie* was the "double duchess," Frances Howard, "Duchesse of Richmond and Lenox," England's wealthiest woman. Within the dedication, Smith celebrated the four other women who "offered me rescue and protection in my greatest dangers," including of course Pocahontas. If the Pocahontas episode were a lie, Smith would have been gratuitously insulting the duchess.

Except for a specially printed dedication page (3:12), both *An Accidence* (1626) and *A Sea Grammar* (1627) have only general dedications. *The True Travels* (1630), however, is extremely revealing. It is dedicated to three noblemen: William Herbert, earl of Pembroke, perhaps the richest Englishman of his day; Robert Bertie, earl of Lindsey; and Henry Carey, earl of Dover. As I pointed out in chapter 2, Herbert would have arranged the presentation of Pocahontas at court and would have met Smith when Smith presented his letter to Queen Anne. At any rate, Herbert, a major investor in both the Virginia Company and the New England Company, certainly knew Smith, and Herbert, as lord chamberlain, must have known of the Pocahontas episode at least since 1616.

In *The True Travels* Smith tells his most incredible story—the defeat of three Turkish champions in single combat. Though he may not have known either Herbert or Carey very well, it seems incredible to think he would falsify his comparatively unimportant Virginia adventures in a book featuring his great eastern European triumphs—and defeats. The third dedicatee, Robert Bertie (1582–1642), was the son of Peregrine Bertie, Lord Willoughby, Smith's local lord. Robert Bertie had known Smith all his life. Smith's father, George Smith, left Peregrine Bertie "the best of my two yeares old colts" in his will and charged and commanded his son John "to honore and love my foresaide good Lord *Willoughbie* duringe his lyfe" (*CW* 3:377).

After his early soldiering in the Lowlands, Smith had returned home, to Willoughby in Lincolnshire, whence he set off in the summer of 1599 with Peregrine Bertie, Jr., younger brother of Robert Bertie. (Peregrine's license to travel was granted on June 26, 1599.) Smith met Robert Bertie at Orléans, France, in the late summer of 1599 (3:155) and again in Siena, Italy, in 1601 (3:161). He must have seen Robert Bertie at

Willoughby and in London off and on throughout his entire life. If Smith had lied about his adventures, Robert Bertie, who became Lord Willoughby de Eresby in 1601 upon his father's death, would certainly have heard about it. If Smith had been a fraud, Bertie would have had nothing to do with him, but Bertie remained Smith's friend and patron throughout Smith's life. As Philip L. Barbour wrote: "Robert Bertie or his shade seems to be standing by at nearly every event in John Smith's eventful life." As Barbour shows in *The Three Worlds*, Bertie knew and was related to many Virginia Company adventurers.[70] Bertie must have heard of Smith's various adventures from many different sources.

One can hardly believe that these persons would have allowed Smith to dedicate books to them if Smith were known to have lied or were suspected of lying about the Pocahontas episode. Evidently the dedicatees of his books had no reason to think him a liar.

Friends of Smith

Two of Smith's closest friends were Sir Samuel Saltonstall and Sir Humphrey Mildmay. Smith lived for some time during the 1620s with each of them. Of the two, Saltonstall, who was knighted at Whitehall on July 23, 1603, seems to have been especially important.[71] Smith says in the dedication of *The True Travels* (1630) that Saltonstall caused his *Sea Grammar* (1627) to be printed (3:142). This may simply mean that Saltonstall encouraged him to write it, or it may mean that Saltonstall paid for its printing. At any rate, Saltonstall contributed commendatory verses to Smith's *Sea Grammar* and there called him familiarly, "Jack Smith" (3:53). I also believe that the six lines of verse under Smith's portrait in the map of New England published in *A Description of New England* are by Saltonstall (the initials *SS* are in the margin by the poem). An additional couplet, which is set off by the lines enclosing the portrait, is by John Davies. Smith evidently considered Saltonstall's home his own London home. In his will, Smith referred to a "trunk standing in my chamber at Sir Samuel Saltonstall's house in St. Sepulchre's Parish" (*CW* 3:383).

Smith knew Saltonstall's family well. He refers to an expedition by his son Captain Charles Saltonstall (3:230). The other son, Wye, contributed commendatory verses for Smith's *Sea Grammar* (3:52) and became himself an authority on navigation.[72] And Sir Samuel's wife's sister married John Hagthorpe, another contributor of prefatory verses to the *Sea Grammar* (3:51). It is not known who paid for the marble tablet erected in St. Sepulchre's Church "To the living memory of his deceased friend Captain John Smith," but Sir Samuel Saltonstall is a good possibility. Whoever did it and wrote the verse certainly believed the extraordinary feats of Smith (3:390).

Smith wrote his last book, *Advertisements for the Unexperienced Planters of New England* (1631) while staying at Danbury Place, Sir Humphrey Mildmay's estate in Essex, a day's ride from London. Sir Humphrey was knighted at Whitehall on July 10, 1616.[73] Smith's appreciation for landscapes and rural scenery emerges clearly in his recommendation that areas of virgin forest in America be preserved. Americans should try to create beautifully landscaped garden areas, "like unto the high grove or tuft of trees, upon the high hill by the house of that worthy Knight Sir Humphrey Mildmay, so remarkable in Essex in the Parish of Danbury, where I writ this discourse," though in America the trees were taller and grander (3:289).

Besides Purchas, two other men of extraordinary learning were good friends of Smith. Sir Robert Bruce Cotton was

knighted on May 11, 1603, at the Charterhouse, along with Sir
Edwin Sandys, later treasurer of the Virginia Company.[74] Cotton, the great collector of English historical manuscripts, was
a friend and admirer of Smith. Smith wrote his *True Travels*
at Cotton's request (3:141). Cotton's librarian, Richard James,
contributed a prefatory poem to the book (3:146–47). Like Sir
Edwin Sandys, Cotton was a member of the Virginia Company. Since he spoke in Parliament against Sandys, Cotton
certainly knew Sandys.[75] Moreover, since Cotton was a naval
expert, he probably knew several commissioners who investi-
gated the Virginia Company in 1623. John Chamberlain said
that one group of five knights, of whom four served on the
Jones commission, were "employed about the matters of the
houshold and navie." The historical and scholarly interests of
Sir William Jones himself make it almost certain that Cotton would have known him.[76] The member of the Jones commission whom Cotton knew especially well, however, was Sir
Henry Bourchier. He turns up repeatedly in Kevin Sharpe's
biography of Cotton. Cotton had ample opportunity to learn
all the facts and rumors about Captain John Smith.

Cotton also knew John Tradescant, another great collector of books and curiosities, who also belonged to the Virginia Company.[77] Smith left Tradescant one quarter of his
books (3:383). Tradescant too must have been Smith's good
friend. John Taylor, the water poet, and Robert Norton, artil-
lery expert, both asked Smith to write dedicatory poems for
their books (3:369–79). They would not have done so if they
thought or if they had heard that Smith was a liar. Close friends
like Saltonstall and Cotton, each of whom was in some way
responsible for one of Smith's late books, obviously respected
and admired Smith. Cotton would not have asked Smith to
write *The True Travels* if he thought Smith was a liar. Sir Samuel

Saltonstall, Sir Humphrey Mildmay, Sir Robert Bruce Cotton, John Tradescant, John Taylor, and Robert Norton all knew Smith well and evidently judged him a man of honor.

Satires on Smith

The *Southern Literary Messenger* reviewer wrote in 1862 that "Captain Smith, who is charged by Mr. Deane with fabricating the story of his rescue, (a story from which *he* could derive no honor, but only Pocahontas,) was often the subject of envy and detraction in his own day, yet his integrity was fully endorsed by his contemporaries." That, however, was not the whole case, and Henry Adams, in his first revision of his attack on Smith, pointed out that Thomas Fuller, in *The History of the Worthies of England* (1662), had impugned Smith. Fuller said that "the scene whereof [of his Balkan and Middle Eastern adventures] is laid at such a distance, they are cheaper credited than confuted" and that "such his perils, preservations, dangers, deliverances [of his American adventures], they seem to most men above belief, to some beyond truth."[78] Adams was right. No one in 1871 had carefully examined the story of Smith's eastern European adventures, and when Adams again revised his attack in 1891, he no doubt felt vindicated, because Lewis L. Kropf had supposedly proven in the previous year that Smith lied about them. But that great comfort to those who wished to discredit Smith vanished in 1953 under Laura Polanyi Striker's blistering attack on Kropf. Further, after the publication of a number of reports by contemporaries who were present in Smith's Virginia, no one now doubts that all his American adventures occurred — with the exception, of course, of the escapade being considered, the Pocahontas episode.

Lawrence C. Wroth first noticed that a popular seventeenth-century satire, David Lloyd's *The Legend of Captaine Iones*, seemed to mock Smith's adventures, particularly those recounted in his *True Travels*.[79] Lloyd's *Legend of Captaine Iones* was entered in the Stationers' Register on May 26, 1631, just over a month before Smith's death on June 21 and well over a year after the publication of Smith's *True Travels*, which was entered in the Stationers' Register on August 29, 1629, with the title page dated 1630 (3:250). Since Lloyd's popular satire went through five editions during Fuller's lifetime, though not all readers would have recognized the butt as Captain John Smith, Fuller may have had Lloyd's *Legend* in mind when he referred to the skepticism of readers concerning Smith's adventures.[80] Lloyd's low burlesque does indeed demonstrate that Smith's numerous adventures were, as we know from Smith's own testimony, burlesqued in his own day, but it proves nothing about the credibility of the adventures themselves.[81]

Indeed, many more burlesques of Smith and Pocahontas appeared in the 1840s, due to the popularity on the American stage of the Indian dramas, than after the attacks by Charles Deane, Henry Adams, Edward D. Neill, Alexander Brown, and Lewis L. Kropf proved to most people that Smith was a liar.[82] But the fashions of parody have no laws.

Though Lawrence C. Wroth called attention to Lloyd's burlesque, he was one of the few scholars of the first half of the twentieth century to believe that Smith might yet be proven to be accurate, and in Smith's defense, Wroth cited a number of contemporary "learned men" who obviously believed Smith's validity. Laura Polanyi Striker has added to the list with her translation of Henry Wharton, *The Life of John Smith, English Soldier*. Wroth was concerned with Smith's Balkan adventures, rather than with the Pocahontas episode, but the same reasoning applies to the American escapade. That some writers and satirists among Smith's contemporaries made use of the redoubtable Smith says nothing about his credibility. It only shows that he was not a rich aristocrat, with a wealthy family to reward those who would sing his praises.[83]

The Character of Smith

Dozens of contemporaries testified that Smith was extraordinarily honest and truthful. Not one of his critics and enemies denied it. His enemies disliked him because of his comparatively egalitarian positions, especially his refusal to accept the automatic superiority of his "social betters." Scholars, from the anonymous 1862 reviewer and Edward Arber to Philip L. Barbour, have emphasized that nothing that Smith wrote has been found to be a lie. In *The American Dream of Captain John Smith*, I have made an extended study of his character and idealism. To think that he lied about the Pocahontas episode and that he continued and repeated the lie throughout the latter part of his life is to ignore not only the evidence from Smith's contemporaries but also all the evidence of his character from his own writings.

If he lied about the Pocahontas episode, then his whole life and his entire presentation of himself and his values were lies. But his life and his writings are of a piece. They testify to his adventuresome idealism. I believe he was absolutely sincere and truthful when he wrote, "Honour is our lives ambition":

> Then seeing we are not borne for our selves, but each to helpe
> other, and our abilities are much alike at the houre of our birth,
> and the minute of our death: Seeing our good deedes, or our

badde, by faith in Christs merits, is all we have to carrie our soules to heaven, or hell: Seeing honour is our lives ambition; and our ambition after death, to have an honourable memorie of our life: and seeing by no means wee would bee abated of the dignities and glories of our Predecessors; let us imitate their vertues to bee worthily their successors. (1:361)

Conclusion

There are eight unmistakable references in Smith's writings to Pocahontas's saving his life. The circumstances of five— the 1616 letter to the queen, the 1622 *New Englands Trials*, the 1623 testimony before the commissioners, the main account in *The Generall Historie*, and the reference in *The True Travels*— make it seem certain that if we had only one of these accounts, we would nevertheless have excellent evidence that Pocahontas saved his life. The overall evidence supplied by all eight (and possibly nine) references proves beyond a shadow of a doubt that Pocahontas rescued him.

Additional confirmation exists. Numerous Indians were present at the ceremony. Some must have lived until at least the time of Opechancanough's death in 1644. Like Opechancanough himself, these Indians could have been asked about the Pocahontas episode, if there was any reason at all to doubt it. If anyone did ask the Indians, they evidently confirmed the story, for no one in the seventeenth century ever specifically questioned it. Further, Smith and Pocahontas both behaved as if a special relationship existed between them after Smith's captivity. The best explanation for the special relationship is that Pocahontas saved (or appeared to save) his life. Many old Virginia hands, including several enemies who must have known the truth, were alive after Smith's story of being rescued by Pocahontas appeared in 1622 and 1624. If any of the old Virginia hands doubted him, they would have spread the word that he was lying.

Samuel Purchas, the foremost scholarly authority on Virginia colonization, made it his business to know all the old Virginia hands and to know everything that went on concerning Virginia. Purchas believed Smith and reprinted the story of his captivity and of being saved by Pocahontas in the 1625 *Hakluytus Posthumus*. Purchas knew and talked with Smith's enemies, including George Percy, Francis West, and Edward Maria Wingfield, but he told the story of Virginia's earliest years from Smith's point of view. Obviously he never heard anything from Smith's friends or enemies that made him think Smith was lying.

If Smith lied about the Pocahontas incident, then he also lied about the 1616 letter to Queen Anne. Adams claimed that there was no such letter or that it did not contain the information that Pocahontas saved Smith's life. But almost the entire court circle, including Prince Charles and Lord Pembroke (who had been lord chamberlain in 1616 and in charge of the affairs at court) would have known about the letter and would have recognized the falsehood. Prince Charles and Lord Pembroke both allowed Smith to dedicate later books to them. It is incredible to think that they would have allowed Smith to do so if he had lied. So too, Smith mentioned before the Jones commission investigating the Virginia Company that Pocahontas had rescued him. Since the commission was in the process of interviewing all the old Virginia hands and all the London Company of Virginia authorities, they would quickly have learned if he were lying to them.

Finally, numerous men of honor were friends of Smith. It is obvious that they respected and admired him. Sir Samuel Saltonstall, Sir Humphrey Mildmay, and Sir Robert Bruce Cotton were among Smith's close friends and were his patrons. At least two well-known contemporaries asked him to write commendatory verses for them. It is obvious that neither they nor anyone else in Smith's day thought that he lied about the Pocahontas episode. If he had lied, they would have learned about it.

Another consideration—if Smith was a liar, he was a remarkably consistent liar over a long period of time. If Pocahontas did not save him, if he did not defeat three Turkish champions successively in single combat, if he did not kill his master when he was a slave in Turkey and make his way across the desert of Russia, or if he did not escape from French pirates by setting off alone in a small boat at night during a tempest that wrecked the pirates' ship, then he possessed an extraordinarily fertile imagination, a Defoe-like genius for realistic details, and a feeling for archetypes comparable to Homer. If his tales are his own imaginative creation, then he is a greater writer of fiction than anyone has ever suspected.[1]

Though I have added a number of considerations to William Wirt Henry's refutation of Henry Adams, I hope that I have also proven that Henry effectively refuted Adams in 1875. Adams's subsequent revisions countered some of the points of the anonymous *Southern Literary Messenger* reviewer and Henry, but many of them went unchallenged. Anyone who thinks that the Pocahontas episode did not happen must believe that Smith's enemies, as well as his friends and acquaintances and others whom he did not know, all conspired with him in keeping the truth of the Pocahontas episode a secret.

By any reasoning, we must conclude that Charles M. Andrews was right when he, without presenting his reasons, said that the Pocahontas story "can be shown to be true in all probability." I hope that I have ended the "Great Debate," as Bradford Smith called the controversy over the Pocahontas episode.[2]

It actually happened.

Henry Adams and Captain John Smith

Though the information in this brief afterword repeats material scattered throughout the text, perhaps it will be useful to gather together a record of Henry Adams's fallacies in his attack on Smith. Adams wrote it—and he also meant it to be an attack upon Pocahontas—in 1862 as war propaganda. He called it a kind of "flank attack" upon the South. As I have pointed out in specific instances in chapter 2, he made two fundamental historiographic errors in his general approach. First, he anachronistically assumed that the Pocahontas episode was especially important to Smith's contemporaries. It was not. The nineteenth-century romancers gave it the mythic importance that it assumed in the minds of Charles Deane, Henry Adams, and other middle and late nineteenth-century historians. Second, Adams approached Smith's writings as if Smith were a "scientific" historian of the mid–nineteenth century, seizing upon such minor discrepancies in Smith's reports as how many men the food he was given would feed. Smith and his contemporaries would have been amazed at such persnicketiness. Any good student of Renaissance literature, like Henry David Thoreau, Ralph Waldo Emerson, or Edward Arber, knew better. Renaissance writers cared little about what they considered to be unimportant details and viewed reality through the lenses of chivalric fiction. Adams, however, thought scientific accuracy in historical writing was possible and desirable.

Adams misrepresented Smith several times. I would like to think that these were inadvertent or careless errors, but it is the nature of propaganda to slant the truth in order to make a point. He was simply wrong in claiming that Smith did not express fear for his life in telling the story of his captivity in *A True Relation* (1608). Writing about *A Map of Virginia* (1612), where an indirect reference to the Pocahontas episode may be found, Adams conflated Smith's description of the Powhatan Indians' three methods of capital punishment and his description of their ordinary method of punishment and sarcastically claimed that the ordinary punishment (beating someone senseless with a cudgel) inspired Smith's description of what was about to happen to him when Pocahontas saved him. Revising the essay in 1891, having forgotten some of the details of what he had read, Adams said that the East Coast Indians rarely, if ever, executed people by beating out their brains. He misrepresented Smith in 1867, and he was simply wrong in his 1891 revision.

His discussion of the 1616 letter to the queen mentioned three people who had died before the publication of the letter in 1624, as if those three constituted the entire court circle. Adams knew better, but he chose to ignore the facts. After William Wirt Henry destroyed this argument in 1875, Adams did not change it in his 1891 revision. Instead, he persisted in an illogical and partial argument. If Adams noticed that the publication of *A Description of New England* (1616) and Prince Charles's change of Indian names occurred just after Pocahontas's arrival in England, he did not say so.

Following a mistake by Charles Deane, Adams bitterly condemned Smith for supposedly blaming John Robinson and Thomas Emry for disobeying orders and for cowardice. The mistake was due to a careless reading and an overeager wish to find fault with Smith. After William Wirt Henry pointed out the error in 1875, Adams silently dropped the charge in 1891, giving Henry no credit and implicitly pretending that the essay remained the same. Adams also chose to ignore the fact that Smith specifically called upon four old Virginia hands who were present in London in 1622 to corroborate his story of subduing Opechancanough, though it was on the same page that he first mentioned in print the Pocahontas episode. Adams deliberately suppressed germane evidence.

Adams also ignored Smith's reference to Pocahontas's saving him in his testimony before the commissioners investigating the Virginia Company in 1623. Though William Wirt Henry mentioned it in his 1882 address to the Virginia Historical Society, Adams did not add the information to his 1891 revision. Again, he deliberately suppressed evidence that tended to refute his position. He did, however, try to deny the special relationship argument that William Wirt Henry made in his 1882 lecture. But by 1891 Adams had forgotten that *The Proceedings* (1612) reported exactly what he blamed *A True Relation* for not saying: Smith pretended to save the Paspaheghs "only" because Pocahontas asked the favor. Further, we know from Adams's personal correspondence in 1861 that he considered the special relationship a reason to believe that Pocahontas did save Smith, but Adams concealed any hint of this contrary argument in 1867 and specifically tried to deny it in 1891.

Afterword

Another Adams error, perhaps due to a mistake in his notes, was his attempt to discredit the Smith-Pocahontas episode by saying that Purchas introduced numerous additional references to Pocahontas in his 1617 edition of *Purchas His Pilgrimage* and that if she had saved Smith, the story would certainly have been introduced there. But in fact Adams quoted from the 1625 *Hakluytus Posthumus* (the 1617 edition had practically no new information), and he suppressed the pertinent evidence that Purchas reprinted the entire Pocahontas episode in 1625. Adams was not only overeager to condemn Smith, but he deliberately overlooked pertinent evidence. Of course, he ignored the presence in London in 1624 of a number of old Virginia hands who would have known about the Pocahontas episode and would have attacked Smith if it had not been true.

I must conclude that Adams deliberately ignored information and arguments that tended to confirm the Pocahontas story, that he suppressed his own doubts and pertinent evidence in order to write good propaganda, that he was, at best, ungracious to William Wirt Henry, that he was careless about facts, that he was overeager to condemn Smith, and that he persisted in reinforcing his anti-Southern propaganda even in 1891. The best that can be said of Adams's essay on Captain John Smith is that Adams wrote excellent anti-Southern propaganda. He committed, however, the numerous faults characteristic of propaganda. As I showed in the introduction, the attack on Smith was intended to vilify the descendants of Pocahontas, to denigrate the Virginians' pride in their early history, and— almost incidentally—to blacken the reputation of Captain John Smith. The assault on Smith was simply South-baiting.

Notes

Introduction

1. See Hayes, *Captain John Smith*, for all references mentioned in the introduction.
2. Levenson et al., eds., *Letters* 1:287.

One. *History of the Dispute*

1. Adams, "Captain John Smith" (1867), 14; Henry, "Rescue."
2. A fair copy of Adams's manuscript from which the 1867 article was set exists at the Houghton Library, bMS Am 1899 (9). It contains a conclusion (comprising the last two lines on p. 37 and all of p. 38) that is not in the article. Ten passages (from a few words to several lines) are also different from the article. Perhaps Adams made these changes in the galleys. Adams thoroughly revised the essay for reprinting in Charles F. Adams, Jr., and Henry Adams, *Chapters of Erie, and Other Essays* (Boston: Osgood and Co., 1871), 192–224; rpt., New York: H. Holt, 1886; Ithaca, N.Y.: Great Seal Books, 1956; Ithaca, N.Y.: Cornell University Press, 1966; New York: A. M. Kelley, 1967.

The essay was reprinted separately as *Pocahontas and Captain John Smith* in the Monograph Series, "a serial collection of indexed essays" (Bangor, Maine: Q. P. Index, 1881). See Blanck, 1:4 (H. Adams no. 13).

Adams again thoroughly revised it for reprinting in Henry Adams, *Historical Essays* (New York: Charles Scribner's Sons, 1891), 42–79.

The 1891 text is reprinted in Stevenson, ed., *A Henry Adams Reader*, 24–57, where the editor, evidently unaware that Adams had extensively revised the essay in 1871 and again in 1891, wrote, "This was his first mature piece of work. In it he wrote in his own style for the first time: a fastidious lightness and elegance caressing an irreproachable solidity of fact." Of course, the essay is also well known from its mention in Adams's classic autobiography, *The Education of Henry Adams* (1907).

3. Henry, "Settlement." Though David Beers Quinn listed William Wirt Henry's 1875 essay in the bibliography prepared for Philip L. Barbour's edition of Smith's *Complete Works* (3:411), Barbour commented in his note on the Pocahontas episode that refutations of Adams "began in 1882" (1:103 n. 123), evidently referring to Henry's "Settlement," his Virginia Historical Society lecture.

4. Adams, *Education*, 222.

5. Palfrey, *History* 1:89n. Palfrey's revised *Compendious History* says that "many of the incidents that are recorded [by Smith] are not to be received without caution" (1:8).

6. Deane, ed., "Discourse," 92–95n.

7. Morse, "John Smith," 123.

8. Morse, "John Smith," 123 and 134n. He discussed W. W. Henry's reply on p. 128, citing only Henry's "Early Settlement" (i.e., "The Settlement at Jamestown, with Particular Reference to the Late Attacks upon Captain John Smith, Pocahontas, and John Rolfe"). In replying to Neill and others as well as to Adams, Henry dissipated the force of his argument, though he did add a few details (the most important of which I will point out below) to his 1875 essay. Henry was Smith's major Southern defender. Henry replied later to the criticisms of Alexander Brown with "A Defense of Captain John Smith" (1891), and again, to a criticism by Neill, with "Did Percy Denounce Smith's History of Virginia?" (1893–94).

9. Morse, "John Smith," 134n.

10. Perhaps she actually prevented his execution; more likely she

sponsored him in a ritualistic death and rebirth into tribal membership. When I write that Pocahontas saved Smith, I mean that the actions Smith described really took place.

11. Stevenson, 24; Safer, 50–68; Malloy, 160–72; Young, 175; Rule, 177, 179; Adams, *Education*, 607.

12. Morse, review, 725–26; Whitehill, 304–5.

13. Davis, review, 697; Hall, 760; Barbour, "Pocahontas," 79.

14. Slaughter, 220.

15. Sheehan, 737.

16. Axtell, 1302; Sheridan, 11; Vaughan, *American Genesis*, 37; Vaughan, "Beyond Pocahontas," 28.

17. Vaughan, "John Smith Satirized," 713. Vaughan concluded, however, that "the current scholarly consensus that Smith's tales are tall but essentially true is unshaken" (732). My own review, "The Voice of Captain John Smith," stressed Smith's general truthfulness and his rehabilitation because of the researches into his accounts of eastern Europe.

18. Jameson, 11–12. Osgood wrote: "On the most famous of his journeys up the Chickahominy, two of his companions were slain. Four weeks elapsed before he was able to return to Jamestown" (1:48–49).

19. Morison, 8.

20. Wroth, 77.

21. Neill, *Virginia Company*; Neill, *English Colonization*; Brown, *Genesis*; Brown, *First Republic*; Brown, *English Politics*.

22. Craven, *Dissolution*, 4–5, 295–98. Craven spends pp. 12–23 refuting Brown's interpretation. See also Craven, *Southern Colonies*, 72–73.

23. Andrews, 1:142n. Morse's essay even influenced Wesley Frank Craven, who wrote, "Whether Pocahontas actually saved his life as he later claimed is not particularly important" (*Southern Colonies*, 72). In a dissenting voice, Kate Mason Rowland dismissed Brown's work and said that William Wirt Henry's 1882 address was "a thorough and

complete vindication of Captain John Smith" against the charges of Henry Adams (118), but no one since has cited her evaluation, which in my opinion is accurate.

24. Striker, "Captain John Smith's Hungary," 333.

25. See Deane, ed., *True Relation*, 38–40n, for Deane's attack on Smith.

26. Like most scholars, Deane and Adams consider *The Proceedings* to be part 2 of *A Map of Virginia*.

27. Deane, ed., "Discourse," 94n, 94–95n.

28. Levenson et al., eds., *Letters* 1:258–59.

29. Deane's letter to Palfrey concerning Adams's search is printed in Cater, 11–12.

30. Levenson et al., eds., *Letters* 1:287. Wyndham Robertson, reviewing Deane in 1860, explained that the common Renaissance meaning of *wanton* was "playful." Rule points out the anti-Southern bias of Henry Adams throughout his life, discussing especially his essay "Captain John Smith" and his biography *John Randolph*.

31. Levenson et al., eds., *Letters* 1:506, 507, 508, 510.

32. Robertson, "Marriage." I cite the *Historical Magazine* text, where the reply to Deane (who is not named) occurs on pp. 295–96. Robertson also examined the Pocahontas episode in *Pocahontas*, 6–13, but there he uses a descendant's hagiographic tones.

33. Unfortunately, neither Benjamin Blake Minor nor David K. Jackson identifies the author of the review. Charles Campbell and William Gilmore Simms are among the candidates for authorship.

34. Levenson et al., eds., *Letters* 1:560.

35. Samuels, 154. Adams remarked that the *Pall Mall Gazette*, in February 1867, devoted a long notice to his essay and that numerous newspaper comments on the piece appeared both in America and "here" in England. Levenson et al., eds., *Letters* 1:520, 521.

36. *The Nation*, January 17, 1867, p. 48.

37. Levenson et al., eds., *Letters* 2:320, 321.

Two. *The Pocahontas Episode in Smith's Writings*

1. Though I refer to Pocahontas's saving Smith as a story or an episode, both terms aggrandize its appearance in Smith's writings. Its most detailed version occurs as a part of one sentence in *The Generall Historie*, quoted in the prologue to this book. *Allusion* or *glimpse* would really be more appropriate terms than *story* or *episode*.

2. All references to Smith's writings are to Philip L. Barbour, ed., *The Complete Works of Captain John Smith*. When the citation might be confusing, I use the abbreviation *CW* to refer to Barbour's edition.

3. Robertson, "Marriage," 296; "Smith's Rescue," 626–27; Henry, "Rescue," 591–92. See *CW* 1:53 n. 126.

4. Mossiker, 84.

5. Deane, ed., "Discourse," 93n.

6. Deane, "Pocahontus and Captain Smith," 494.

7. Deane, ed., "Discourse," 93n.

8. Adams, "Captain John Smith" (1867), 11; (1871), 202–3; (1891), 54. This method of citing Adams will be used hereafter when the presence or absence of revisions seems important. The original publication in the *North American Review* will be cited as 1867, the revised version in *Chapters of Erie* will be cited as 1871, and the final revision in the *Historical Essays* will be cited as 1891. The version quoted will be listed first.

9. "Smith's Rescue," 628. The anonymous author cited the following passage: "That night they quartered in the woods, he [Smith] still expecting, (as he had done all this long time of his imprisonment) every hour to be put to one death or other, for all their feasting." But it is from *The Generall Historie* (2:151).

10. Strachey, 59–60.

11. Even diarists, necessarily selecting the particulars they choose to record, betray a teleological purpose.

12. For a survey of the changing relations between Smith and Powhatan and for some suggestions about the difference in their relations after Smith learned that the Powhatans killed the Roanoke colonists,

see Lemay, *American Dream*, 145–66.

13. Robertson, "Marriage," 296; Henry, "Rescue," 524–25.

14. Wingfield himself is the authority for the trial and fine. Barbour, ed., *Jamestown Voyages*, 223. (The two volumes are paginated continuously.)

15. Bradford Smith, 117.

16. Henry, "Rescue," 525.

17. Ibid.

18. Bradford Smith, 116.

19. For example, what happened to the Indian who was left with Robinson and Emry? The two whites were killed, but the Indian is not mentioned. What happened to the Indian guide who was with Smith when he was captured? Smith used the guide as a shield when attacked, and later the guide arranged for Smith to surrender. Smith never mentioned him again. What became of the extraordinary Anas Todkill, who risked his life to save the expedition? Did he return to England with Smith?

20. In 1884 Edward Arber objected to critics who called Smith vain: "Evidently his personal adventures are rather understated than overstated therein [in *The True Travels*]. He was surely not idle on board the Breton ship, in that fight in 1601, in the Strait of Otranto, when she took the Venetian argossy, *pp.* 826–7; or in that other sea-fight in 1604, off Cape Bojador, when the English ship (in which, by stress of weather, he made an involuntary cruise), under the command of Captain Merham, whom he so delightedly calls 'the old fox,' fought two Spanish men-of-war at once, *pp.* 878–80: yet of the personal help, which we are sure he gave on both these occasions, he says not a word. So generally, while he is proud of his strategy and devices, he tells us very little of his personal bravery in the various battles in Eastern Europe in which he took part: with the exception of the succession of duels that he fought at Regal in 1602" (Arber and Bradley 1:xxii).

21. Barbour, ed., *Jamestown Voyages*, 227.

22. Robertson, "Marriage," 295.

23. For surveys of later writers who used Smith, see Wecter, 17–25, 493; Hubbell; and Young.

24. Strachey, 59–60. Strachey praises Smith after referring to his map, saying, "Of whose paynes taken herein, I leave to the Censure of the Reader to Iudge. Sure I am, there will not returne from thence in hast, any one who hath bene more industrious, or who hath had (Captain George Percy excepted) greater experyence amongest them, however misconstruction may traduce him here at home, where is not easly seene the mixed sufferaunces both of body and mynd, which is there daily, and with no few hazardes, and hearty griefes vndergone" (49–50).

25. Barbour notes that William White, who was living with the Indians at the time, told Purchas that he witnessed Cassen's execution. Perhaps, as Barbour suggests, White told Smith of Cassen's execution, though I see no reason to doubt Smith, who says he learned about it from the Indians (1:175 n. 10).

26. Adams, "Captain John Smith" (1867), 20; (1871), 213; (1891), 65–66. The basic content of this passage was not revised.

27. Adams wrote to Palfrey on October 23, 1861, and said that Smith's "first published account of it was printed I believe in 1612, only five years afterward." Either Adams was mistaken or he was referring to the indirect reference in *A Map*. Both the fact that he had just read through Smith looking for evidence against the Smith-Pocahontas episode and his attempt to refute this possible allusion in his finished essay suggest that he had the allusion in mind. Of course Deane replied that Smith's earliest accounts contained no reference to the episode. Levenson et al., eds., *Letters* 1:258, 281 n. 1.

28. Smith says that she arrived at Plymouth on June 12, 1616 (2:255), but Thomas Dale, with whom she sailed, wrote Ralfe Wynwood from Plymouth on June 3, 1616. Brown, *Genesis*, 783–84. Samuel Purchas dates their arrival at Plymouth "in May or June 4, 1616" (*Hakluytus Posthumus* 19:117).

29. Levenson et al., eds., *Letters* 1:259.

30. Ibid., 280. Palfrey's note to Deane and Deane's reply are printed in Cater, 11–12n.

31. Deane, ed., "Discourse," 94n; "Smith's Rescue," 628, 629.

32. Adams, "Captain John Smith" (1867), 28. Adams, "Captain John Smith" (1871), 221; (1891), 76; cf. (1867), 28.

33. Henry, "Rescue," 595.

34. Ibid.

35. Kingsbury 3:86, 331.

36. Ibid., 480, 587. See also the *DNB* entry on Herbert.

37. Adams, "Captain John Smith" (1867), 26–27; (1871), 220.

38. Henry, "Rescue," 527. Strachey, 60, supplies the reason the men disobeyed orders and went ashore.

39. Compare the paragraph following the quotation from Smith in Adams, "Captain John Smith" (1867), 26–27 (reprinted in [1871], 220), with its version in (1891), 75.

40. Henry, "Rescue," 595.

41. The exact date of Smith's testimony is unknown. The commission gathered testimony from May 9 into early June 1623. Craven, *Dissolution*, 295. Rymer printed the committee's official charge, 17:490–92.

42. Craven, *Dissolution*, prints "Fortesan," an error for Fortescue.

43. Ibid., 267.

44. Henry, "Settlement," 56.

45. Though listed in Lemon, 61, no. 209, it was generally unknown until reprinted in a facsimile, edited by Luther S. Livingston in 1914.

46. *Biographical Sketches* (1828), 27; 2d ed. (1829), 27. Hunt 1:96.

47. Deane, ed., *True Relation*, 40n.

48. Levenson et al., eds., *Letters* 1:287, 359, 506, 507–8, 510.

49. Hubbell, 184, 185.

50. Emerson, 81.

51. Adams, "Captain John Smith" (1867), 11.

52. Deane, ed., "Discourse," 95n; Adams, "Captain John Smith" (1867), 30, 10.

53. Henry, "Rescue," 528.

54. Ibid., 592.

55. Brown, *Genesis* 2:599, followed Adams in claiming that Smith "continually alters" the details "to his own advantage" in *The Generall Historie*. The example Brown cited is the best one in Smith's writings: in *The Proceedings*, Smith wrote that when the king of Paspahegh attacked him, the king bore him down to the river and attempted to drown him, but two Poles returning from the glass house fell on the king, subduing him (1:260). In the 1624 version, Smith does not mention the Poles but conquers the Paspahegh chief alone (2:209).

56. Morse, "John Smith," 131.

57. Besides the father who tried to kill him because his son lay dying, "wounded with my pistoll," Smith was told of "another I had slayne, yet the most concealed they had any hurte" (1:49). In *The Generall Historie*, he only mentioned the young warrior who was "then breathing his last" (2:148).

58. Robertson, "Marriage," 295; Thoreau 7:108–9; Jewkes, 27; Barbour, "Fact and Fiction," 107; Goodman.

59. McMillan, 96; White.

60. Adams, "Captain John Smith" (1867), 29. Adams wrote to Palfrey: "Your idea was, I think, that the episode was of London Grubstreet manufacture, and the main reason for the doubt, was that Wingfield does not mention Pocahontas in his Diary written at the time, on the spot." Levenson et al., eds., *Letters* 1:258.

61. The most recent editor of Smith seems to agree with Adams: "Smith's later inclusion of stirring adventures such as his rescue by Pocahontas may have been in response to the stimulus of fellow writers who led him away from the goal of the plain unvarnished tale toward that of literary success" (Kupperman, 4).

62. Henry, "Rescue," 596–97.

63. Purchas, *Hakluytus Posthumus* 19:235.

64. Henry, "Rescue," 597.

65. Mossiker, 85. Actually, there are no records of Wiffin after 1616, though his dedicatory verses for Smith (written in collaboration

with the Fettiplaces) were reprinted in *The Generall Historie* (1:317–18; 2:229–30).

66. Sketches of Herbert and Cotton are available in *CW* 1:xxxviii, xxxiii; in Brown, *Genesis* 2:921–22, 865; and in the *DNB*.

67. Brathwait's catalog of four women who had befriended Smith (Tragabigyanda, Callamata's *love*, / *Deare* Pocahontas, *Madam* Shanoi's *Too*, / *Who did what love with modesty could doe*") probably reflects Smith's dedication in *The Generall Historie* (2:41–42), but his spelling of "Madam Shanoi" (cf. Smith's "Madam Chanoyes" [2:42]) suggests that he may have heard the names from Smith.

68. Fuller, 276.

69. One common soldier matched Smith's feat. See the *DNB* account of Richard Pike (or Peake), who in 1625, armed only with a quarterstaff, fought three Spanish soldiers simultaneously, while they were armed with rapiers and poniards.

Three. *Considerations Bearing upon the Dispute*

1. "Sir Thomas Dale is arrived from Virginia and brought with him somme ten or twelve old and younge of that countrie, among whom the most remarquable person is Poco-huntas." Chamberlain (June 22, 1616), 2:10.

2. Barbour, ed., *Jamestown Voyages*, 91–92, 171.

3. Purchas, *Purchas His Pilgrimage* (1613), 641.

4. Fausz, "'Barbarous Massacre' Reconsidered," 21–22.

5. Quoted in "Smith's Rescue," 630.

6. Hodge 1:863, s.v. "Milly."

7. Morse, "John Smith," said that Adams "overstepped the bounds of accuracy, however, in holding that the rescue was contrary to Indian customs and to the known facts of colonial history" (125).

8. Adams, "Captain John Smith" (1891), 66. Cf. (1867), 21; and (1871), 213.

9. Adams, "Captain John Smith" (1867), 20.

10. Purchas, *Purchas His Pilgrimage* (1617), 955; Spelman, in Arber and Bradley 1:cxi.

11. Fletcher, 127–28; Bradford Smith, 118, repeating Fletcher; Barbour, *Pocahontas*, 24–25. Barbour, ed., 1:lxx, said that "Indian customs provide an explanation."

12. Hodge 1:15–16, 592, 863; 2:144–46, s.v. "Adoption," "Huskanaw," "Milly," and "Ordeals." Flannery, 127–28, s.v. "Adopt prisoners." On initiation ceremonies, see Swanton, 712, 815; also Flannery, 94–95.

13. *Virginia Richly Valued*, 22.

14. Fletcher, 127–28, and Bradford Smith, 118, both used the Ortiz story to confirm the Pocahontas episode. Cabell, *Ladies and Gentlemen*, 207–9, suggested that the rescue story was a myth possibly suggested by the Miranda-Ferdinand episode in *The Tempest*. Cabell, in *Let Me Lie*, 51–53, also suggested that Smith was inspired by the Ortiz story.

15. Mossiker, 82–83.

16. Henry, "Rescue," 593; Robertson, "Marriage," 296.

17. Adams, "Captain John Smith" (1891), 55. Cf. (1867), 11; (1871), 203.

18. Adams, "Captain John Smith" (1891), 56.

19. "Smith's Rescue," 630; see *CW* 2:259.

20. Adams, "Captain John Smith" (1871), 214; (1891), 67–68; not in 1867.

21. Adams, "Captain John Smith" (1871), 214; (1891), 67–68; not in 1867. Cf. *CW* 1:274.

22. Adams, "Captain John Smith" (1867), 22; (1871), 214; (1891), 68.

23. The section is signed by Richard Pots and by W.P. Barbour noted, "This is surely for William Phettiplace"; *CW* 1:104. Pots is not known to have been at Werowocomoco, but Fettiplace was. See *CW* 1:55–56 for the persons who accompanied Smith on this expedition.

24. Robertson, "Marriage," 296; "Smith's Rescue," 630.

25. Hamor, 5–6; Barbour, *Pocahontas*, xix.

26. "Smith's Rescue," 630.

27. Levenson et al., eds., *Letters* 1:259.

28. Mossiker, 86.

29. Purchas wrote that his information from Smith came "partly by word of mouth" (*Purchas His Pilgrimage* [1613], 634). He said of the Virginia Indians: "All things that are able to hurt them beyond their preuention, they after their sort adore, as the Fire, Water, Lightning, Thunder, our Ordnance, Peeces, Horses: Yea, Captaine *Smith* told mee, that they seeing one of the English Bores in the way, were stricken with awfull feare, because hee bristled vp himselfe and gnashed his teeth, and tooke him for the God of the Swine, which was offended with them" (639).

30. Purchas, *Purchas His Pilgrimage* (1613), 632.

31. Ibid., 633, 635, 641.

32. Purchas, *Purchas His Pilgrimage* (1614), 757, 768, 759, 761, 768, 759, 766, 759.

33. Purchas, *Purchas His Pilgrimage* (1617), 944, 946.

34. Ibid., 952, 946–48, 954–55.

35. Purchas, *Hakluytus Posthumus* 18:472; 19:118.

36. Ibid. 19:118.

37. Adams, "Captain John Smith" (1867), 25.

38. Ibid. See Purchas, *Purchas His Pilgrimage* (1617), 940.

39. Though not focusing on Smith and Pocahontas, Philip L. Barbour has examined the additions Purchas gradually made to the Virginia materials in the later editions of his works. Barbour, "Samuel Purchas," 44–46.

40. Purchas, *Hakluytus Posthumus* 19:118.

41. Adams, "Captain John Smith" (1867), 13; (1871), 205.

42. Adams, "Captain John Smith" (1891), 58; Levenson et al., eds., *Letters* 1:560; "Smith's Rescue," 629.

43. In revising his essay, Adams deleted the specific reference to the "edition of 1617" ("Captain John Smith" [1867], 25) and made the reference simply: "Yet Purchas's book contained no allusion to the

heroic intervention on behalf of Smith" ([1871], 218; [1891], 73). The paragraph begins, however, with a reference to Purchas's third edition, that is, the 1617 edition, and discusses that edition.

44. Henry, "Rescue," 597.

45. See Purchas, *Hakluytus Posthumus* 18:472.

46. Henry, "Rescue," 525–26; Barbour, ed., *Jamestown Voyages*, 226–27; Strachey, 60, 96–97.

47. Its reputation in American literature began with Robert Beverley's treatment of the episode in his *History and Present State of Virginia*, 39–44. An English correspondent of a colonial American writer used the Pocahontas story to reply to the first recorded complaint about the absence of literary materials in America. In the *Boston Gazette* for June 24, 1734, a correspondent assured his Boston friend that "there's no want of Subjects in that part of the Globe [America]. What a glorious Figure wou'd the Princess Pocahontas make, Painted by a fine hand? How charmingly wou'd she shine interceding with her Rigid Father for the Life of the *English* Captain, and when that wou'd not prevail, throwing her own Neck upon his, and by that means intercepting the Fatal Blow." Then the *Boston Gazette* reprinted Beverley's account. See Towner. The growth of Smith's reputation is splendidly documented in Hayes, *Captain John Smith*.

48. "Smith's Rescue," 630–31; Henry, "Rescue," 596.

49. See Jester and Hiden, 217–18, 507–9, 533–34, 723–26.

50. "Smith's Rescue," 630; Robertson, "Marriage," 295; Henry, "Rescue," 597.

51. Wingfield's "Discourse" in Barbour, ed., *Jamestown Voyages*, 220, 223. Brief biographical sketches, usually with bibliographic references, of all the individuals considered in the next few pages are to be found in Barbour, ed., *CW* 1:xxix–liv.

52. Purchas, *Hakluytus Posthumus* 18:480; cf. 18:530.

53. *CW* 1:273–75; reprinted with revisions in Purchas, *Hakluytus Posthumus* 18:535–37.

54. See Barbour, "Honorable George Percy."

55. Percy, 264.

56. Arber and Bradley 1:cii. For details about West and three of his brothers in Virginia, see Jester and Hiden, 655–61.

57. For three convenient lists of the council members, see Bemiss, 44–45, 85, 125.

58. Craven, *Dissolution*, 38–42.

59. Nichols 1:115.

60. John Smyth of Nibley Papers, Manuscript Division, New York Public Library.

61. Kingsbury, vols. 1 and 2.

62. Chamberlain 1:57. John Rolfe asked that "so liberall a stipend, may not died with my wife, but contynue for her childes advancement." Kingsbury 3:72. Since Purchas saw Uttamatomakkin frequently at Dr. Goulston's, I hypothesize that Goulston was responsible for the Indian visitors.

63. Purchas, *Hakluytus Posthumus* 19:235. Smith's 1614 voyage to New England confirmed this change.

64. Nichols 3:253. The *DNB* mistakenly dates his knighthood March 14, 1617.

65. Nichols 3:487; Chamberlain 2:251, 281, 446.

66. Metcalfe, 175; Nichols 3:526. Both Metcalfe and Nichols give the name as Fortesan, not Fortescue. The *DNB* says that Fortescue was knighted in 1618.

67. The commission is printed in Rymer 17:490–92 and lists Fortescue, not Fortesan.

68. Nichols 3:516; Chamberlain 2:210. Nichols spells William Pitt's surname "Pitte."

69. Nichols 4:732. Bourchier is evidently the same person as the Sir Henry Bourgchier who turns up frequently in Sharpe's biography of Sir Robert Bruce Cotton, for Metcalfe and Nichols give no record of a knight named Sir Henry Bourgchier.

70. Barbour, ed., *CW* 1:xxxi. See Barbour's four genealogies of the Bertie family in *Three Worlds*, 419–21.

71. Nichols 1:209.

72. *DNB*, s.v. "Saltonstall, Wye."

73. Nichols 3:178.

74. Ibid. 1:115.

75. Kingsbury 3:320; Sharpe, 156.

76. Chamberlain 2:210. For Jones's translations, see *Short-Title Catalogue*, 12462, 15701, and 18428. See also the *DNB* article on Jones.

77. Kingsbury 3:58.

78. "Smith's Rescue," 630. Adams, "Captain John Smith" (1871), 221–22, 224; cf. (1891), 76, 79.

79. Wroth, 78.

80. In Fuller's lifetime, editions appeared in 1631, 1636, 1648, 1656, and 1659. See the *National Union Catalog of Pre-1956 Imprints*, nos. NL0427096–NL0427102. Wood claimed that the source of Lloyd's satire was a Welsh poem entitled *Owdt Richard John Greulon*, and the author of the *DNB* entry on Lloyd cited Wood. The most recent biographical notice of Lloyd says that *The Legend of Captaine Iones* is "a good-natured burlesque of the exploits of an Elizabethan seaman. The braggart captain is to be regarded as a type rather than as a real person." *Dictionary of Welsh Biography*, 576, s.v. "J[ohn] J[ames] J[ones]." Although Lloyd was satirizing Smith, he was also using a Welsh burlesque, "Awdl Foliant Rhisiart Sion o Fuellt" (whose first line reads: "Rhisiart Sion grulon, gwroliaeth—Lloegr oll") as a model. Vaughan, "John Smith Satirized."

81. Wrote Smith, "They have acted my fatall Tragedies upon the Stage, and racked my Relations at their pleasure" (3:141). Barbour has suggested that the play, probably by Richard Gunnell, that Smith had in mind was *The Hungarian Lion*, licensed for performance on December 4, 1623. Barbour, "Captain John Smith and the London Theatre." Ben Jonson, of course, introduced Pocahontas in his comedy *The Staple of News* (performed in 1625, published in 1631). Jonson 6:322; 10:272. Wecter, 21–23.

82. Wecter, 21–23.

83. Lanham.

Conclusion

1. Lemay, "Captain John Smith," in *History of Southern Literature*, 31–32.

2. Andrews 1:142n; Bradford Smith, 13.

Bibliography

Adams, Henry. "Captain John Smith." *North American Review* 104 (1867):1–30.

———. "Captain John Smith." In *Chapters of Erie, and Other Essays.* By Charles F. Adams, Jr., and Henry Adams. Boston: Osgood and Co., 1871. 192–224.

———. "Captain John Smith." In *Historical Essays.* By Henry Adams. New York: Charles Scribner's Sons, 1891. 42–79.

———. *The Education of Henry Adams.* Ed. Ernest Samuels. Boston: Houghton Mifflin, 1974.

———. *John Randolph.* Boston: Houghton Mifflin, 1882.

Andrews, Charles M. *The Colonial Period of American History.* 4 vols. New Haven: Yale University Press, 1934.

Arber, Edward, ed. *The Works of Captain John Smith.* Birmingham: English Scholar's Library no. 16, 1884.

Arber, Edward, and A. G. Bradley, eds. *Travels and Works of Captain John Smith.* 2 vols. Edinburgh: John Grant, 1910.

Axtell, James. "Subduing the Wilde Salvages." Review of *The Complete Works of Captain John Smith*, ed. Philip L. Barbour. London *Times Literary Supplement*, November 21, 1986, p. 1302.

Barbour, Philip L. "Captain John Smith and the London Theatre." *Virginia Magazine of History and Biography* 83 (1975):277–79.

———. "Captain John Smith's *True Travels.*" *Bulletin of the New York Public Library* 67 (1963):517–28. Rpt. as "Fact and Fiction in Captain John Smith's *True Travels.*" In *Literature as a Mode of*

Bibliography

Travel. Ed. Warner Rice. New York: New York Public Library, 1963. 101–14.

———. "The Honorable George Percy: Premier Chronicler of the First Virginia Voyage." *Early American Literature* 6 (1971):7–17.

———. "Pocahontas." In *Notable American Women, 1607–1950.* Ed. Edward T. James. 3 vols. Cambridge: Harvard University Press, 1971. 3:78–80.

———. *Pocahontas and Her World.* Boston: Houghton Mifflin, 1970.

———. "Samuel Purchas: The Indefatigable Encyclopedist Who Lacked Good Judgment." In *Essays in Early Virginia Literature Honoring Richard Beale Davis.* Ed. J. A. Leo Lemay. New York: Burt Franklin, 1977. 35–52.

———. *The Three Worlds of Captain John Smith.* Boston: Houghton Mifflin, 1964.

———, ed. *The Complete Works of Captain John Smith.* 3 vols. Chapel Hill: University of North Carolina Press, 1986.

———, ed. *The Jamestown Voyages under the First Charter, 1606–1609.* 2 vols. Hakluyt Society, 2d ser., vols. 136 and 137. Cambridge: Cambridge University Press, 1969.

Bemiss, Samuel M. *The Three Charters of the Virginia Company of London with Seven Related Documents, 1606–1621.* Williamsburg: Jamestown 350th Anniversary Historical Booklet no. 4, 1957.

Beverley, Robert. *History and Present State of Virginia.* 1705. Ed. Louis B. Wright. Chapel Hill: University of North Carolina Press, 1947.

Biographical Sketches of Great and Good Men, Designed for the Amusement and Instruction of Young Persons. Boston: Putnam and Hunt, 1828. 2d ed., Boston: Putnam and Hunt, 1829.

Blanck, Jacob. *Bibliography of American Literature.* 8 vols. New Haven: Yale University Press, 1955–.

Brown, Alexander. *English Politics in Early Virginia.* Boston: Houghton Mifflin, 1901.

———. *The First Republic in America.* Boston: Houghton Mifflin, 1898.

——. *The Genesis of the United States.* 2 vols. Boston: Houghton Mifflin, 1890.

Cabell, James Branch. *Ladies and Gentlemen.* 1934. Rpt., Freeport, N.Y.: Books for Libraries Press, 1968.

——. *Let Me Lie.* New York: Farrar, Straus and Co., 1947.

Carson, Jane. "The Will of John Rolfe." *Virginia Magazine of History and Biography* 58 (1950):58–65.

Cater, Harold Dean, ed. *Henry Adams and His Friends: A Collection of His Unpublished Letters.* Boston: Houghton Mifflin, 1947.

Chamberlain, John. *The Letters of John Chamberlain.* Ed. Norman Egbert McClure. 2 vols. Philadelphia: American Philosophical Society, 1939.

Clayton-Torrence, William. *A Trial Bibliography of Colonial Virginia.* 2 vols. Richmond: Virginia State Library, 1908–10.

C[okayne], G. E. *The Complete Peerage of England, Scotland, Ireland, Great Britain, and the United Kingdom, Extant, Extinct, or Dormant.* Ed. Geoffrey H. White et al. 14 vols. London: St. Catherine Press, 1910–59.

Cole, George Watson, comp. *A Catalogue of Books Relating to the Discovery and Early History of North and South America, Forming a Part of the Library of E. D. Church.* 5 vols. New York: Dodd, Mead, 1907.

Cooper, Gail. *A Checklist of American Imprints for 1830.* Metuchen, N.J.: Scarecrow Press, 1972.

Corbett, Margery, and Ronald Lightbrown. *The Comely Frontispiece: The Emblematic Title Page in England, 1550–1660.* London: Routledge and Kegan Paul, 1979.

Craven, Wesley Frank. *The Dissolution of the Virginia Company: The Failure of a Colonial Experiment.* 1932. Rpt., Gloucester, Mass.: Peter Smith, 1964.

——. *The Southern Colonies in the Seventeenth Century, 1607–1689.* Baton Rouge: Louisiana State University Press, 1949.

Culliford, S. G. *William Strachey, 1572–1621.* Charlottesville: University Press of Virginia, 1965.

Davis, Richard Beale. *Intellectual Life in the Colonial South, 1585–1763.*
3 vols. Knoxville: University of Tennessee Press, 1978.

——. Review of *The Three Worlds of Captain John Smith,* by
Philip L. Barbour. *Journal of American History* 51 (1965):696–98.

Deane, Charles. "Pocahontus and Captain Smith: A Reminiscence."
Magazine of American History with Notes and Queries 13
(1885):492–94.

——, ed. "A Discourse of Virginia." By Edward Maria Wingfield.
In *Archaeologia Americana: Transactions and Collections of the
American Antiquarian Society* 4 (1860):67–103.

——, ed. *A True Relation.* By Captain John Smith. Boston: Wiggin
and Lunt, 1866.

Dictionary of American English. Ed. William Craigie and James R.
Hulbert. 4 vols. Chicago: University of Chicago Press, 1933–44.

*Dictionary of Canadian Biography / Dictionnaire biographique du
Canada.* Ed. George W. Brown and Marcel Trudel. Vol. 1.
Toronto: University of Toronto Press, 1965.

Dictionary of Welsh Biography. Oxford: Blackwell, 1959.

Emerson, Everett. *Captain John Smith.* New York: Twayne, 1971.

*European Americana: A Chronological Guide to Works Printed in Europe
Relating to the Americas.* Ed. John Alden and Dennis C. Landis.
2 vols. (to 1650). New York: Readex Books, 1980–82.

Fausz, Frederick J. "The 'Barbarous Massacre' Reconsidered: The
Powhatan Uprising of 1622 and the Historians." *Explorations in
Ethnic Studies* 1 (January 1978):16–36.

——. "Middlemen in Peace and War: Virginia's Earliest Indian
Interpreters, 1608–1632." *Virginia Magazine of History and
Biography* 95 (1987):41–64.

——. "Opechancanough: Indian Resistance Leader." In *Struggle
and Survival in Colonial America.* Ed. David G. Sweet and Gary B.
Nash. Berkeley: University of California Press, 1981. 21–37.

Flannery, Regina. *An Analysis of Coastal Algonquian Culture.*
Washington, D.C.: Catholic University of America Press, 1939.

Fletcher, John Gould. *John Smith—Also Pocahontas*. New York:
Bretanos, 1928.

Franklin, Benjamin. *Benjamin Franklin: Writings*. Ed. J. A. Leo
Lemay. New York: Library of America, 1987.

Fuller, Thomas. *The History of the Worthies of England*. 1662. Ed.
P. Austin Nuttall. 3 vols. London: T. Tegg, 1840.

Goodman, Jennifer Robin. "The Captain's Self-Portrait: John Smith
as Chivalric Biographer." *Virginia Magazine of History and
Biography* 89 (1981):27–38.

Hakluyt, Richard. *The Principal Navigations, Voyages, Traffiques, and
Discoveries of the English Nation*. 3 vols. London: G. Bishop,
R. Newberie, and R. E. Barker, 1598–1600. Rpt., 12 vols. London:
Hakluyt Society, 1903–5.

Hall, Michael G. Review of *The Three Worlds of Captain John Smith*,
by Philip L. Barbour. *American Historical Review* 70 (1965):759–60.

Hamor, Ralph. *A True Discourse of the Present Estate of Virginia*. 1615.
Ed. A. L. Rowse. Richmond: Virginia State Library, 1957.

Hart, Albert Bushnell. "American Historical Liars." *Harper's
Magazine* 113 (1915):726–35.

Hayes, Kevin J. *Captain John Smith: A Reference Guide*. Boston:
G. K. Hall, 1991.

——. "Defining the Ideal Colonist: Captain John Smith's Revisions
from *A True Relation* to the *Proceedings* to the Third Book of *The
Generall Historie*." *Virginia Magazine of History and Biography* 99
(1991):123–44.

Heilbronner, Walter Leo. "The Earliest Printed Account of the
Death of Pocahontas." *Virginia Magazine of History and Biography*
66 (1958):272–77.

Henry, William Wirt. "A Defense of Captain John Smith."
Magazine of American History 25 (1891):300–313.

——. "Did [George] Percy Denounce Smith's History of
Virginia?" *Virginia Magazine of History and Biography*
1 (1893–94):473–76.

———. "The Rescue of Captain John Smith by Pocahontas." *Potter's American Monthly* 4 (1875):523–28; 5 (1875):591–97.

———. "The Settlement at Jamestown, with Particular Reference to the Late Attacks upon Captain John Smith, Pocahontas, and John Rolfe." Virginia Historical Society *Proceedings* (1882):10–63.

Hodge, Frederick Webb. *Handbook of American Indians North of Mexico.* 2 vols. 1908–10. Rpt., Totowa, N.J.: Rowman and Littlefield, 1979.

Hubbell, Jay B. "The Smith-Pocahontas Story in Literature." *Virginia Magazine of History and Biography* 65 (1957):275–300. Rpt., revised, in *South by Southwest.* By Jay B. Hubbell. Durham, N.C.: Duke University Press, 1965. 175–214.

Hulme, Peter. "John Smith and Pocahontas." In *Colonial Encounters.* By Peter Hulme. New York: Methuen, 1986. 136–73.

Hunt, Freeman. *American Anecdotes.* 2 vols. Boston: Putnam and Hunt, 1830.

Jackson, David K. *The Contributors and Contributions to the Southern Literary Messenger (1834–1864).* Charlottesville, Va.: Historical Publishing Co., 1936.

Jameson, J. Franklin. *The History of Historical Writing in America.* 1891. Rpt., New York: Antiquarian Press, 1961.

Jester, Annie Lash, and Martha Woodroof Hiden, comps. *Adventurers of Purse and Person: Virginia, 1607–1624/5.* 3d ed., revised by Virginia M. Meyer and John Frederick Dorman. Richmond: Dietz Press for the Order of First Families of Virginia, 1987.

Jewkes, William T. "The Literature of Travel and the Mode of Romance in the Renaissance." In *Literature as a Mode of Travel.* Ed. Warner Rice. New York: New York Public Library, 1963. 13–30.

Jonson, Ben. *The Works of Ben Jonson.* Ed. C. H. Herford, Percy Simpson, and Evelyn Simpson. 11 vols. Oxford: Clarendon Press, 1925–52.

Kingsbury, Susan M., ed. *The Records of the Virginia Company of London.* 4 vols. Washington, D.C.: Government Printing Office, 1906–35.

Kropf, Lewis L. "Captain John Smith of Virginia." *Notes and Queries,* 7th ser., 9 (1890):1–2, 41–43, 102–4, 161–62, 223–24, 281–82.

Kupperman, Karen Ordahl, ed. *Captain John Smith: A Select Edition of His Works.* Chapel Hill: University of North Carolina Press, 1988.

Lanham, Richard. "Sidney: The Ornament of His Age." *Southern Review: An Australian Journal of Literary Studies* 2 (1968):319–40.

Lemay, J. A. Leo. *The American Dream of Captain John Smith.* Charlottesville: University Press of Virginia, 1991.

——. "Captain John Smith." In *The History of Southern Literature.* Ed. Louis D. Rubin, Jr., et al. Baton Rouge: Louisiana State University Press, 1985. 26–33.

——. "Captain John Smith: American(?)." *University of Mississippi Studies in English,* n.s., 5 (1984–87):288–96.

——. "The Voice of Captain John Smith." *Southern Literary Journal* 20 (1987):113–31.

Lemon, Robert, comp. *Catalogue of a Collection of Printed Broadsides in the Possession of the Society of Antiquaries of London.* London: Society of Antiquaries, 1866.

Levenson, J. C., Ernest Samuels, Charles Vandersee, and Viola Hopkins Winner, eds. *The Letters of Henry Adams.* 6 vols. Cambridge: Harvard University Press, 1982–88.

L[ivingston], L[uther] S., ed. *The Generall History of Virginia by John Smith.* Facsimile of pamphlet published in London, 1623. Cambridge, Mass.: privately printed, 1914.

Lloyd, David. *The Legend of Captaine Iones.* London: I. M[arriott], 1631.

McMillan, Malcolm C. "Jeffersonian Democracy and the Origins of Sectionalism." In *Writing Southern History: Essays in Historiography in Honor of Fletcher M. Green*. Ed. Arthur S. Link and Rembert W. Patrick. Baton Rouge: Louisiana State University Press, 1965. 91–124.

Malloy, Jeanne M. "William Byrd's Histories and John Barth's *The Sot-Weed Factor*." *Mississippi Quarterly* 42 (1989):160–72.

Mathews, Mitford M., ed. *A Dictionary of Americanisms on Historical Principles*. Chicago: University of Chicago Press, 1951.

Metcalfe, Walter Charles. *A Book of Knights . . . [1642–1660]*. London: Mitchell and Hughes, 1885.

Minor, Benjamin Blake. *The Southern Literary Messenger, 1834–1864*. New York: Neale Publishing Co., 1905.

Morison, Samuel Eliot. *Builders of the Bay Colony*. Boston: Houghton Mifflin, 1930.

Morse, Jarvis M. "John Smith and His Critics: A Chapter in Colonial Historiography." *Journal of Southern History* 1 (1935):123–37.

———. Review of *Captain John Smith: His Life and Legend*, by Bradford Smith. *Mississippi Valley Historical Review* 40 (1954):725–26.

Mossiker, Frances. *Pocahontas: The Life and the Legend*. New York: Knopf, 1976.

Neill, Edward D. *English Colonization of America*. London: Strahan and Co., 1871.

———. *Virginia Company of London*. Albany, N.Y.: J. Munsell, 1869.

Nichols, John. *The Progresses, Processions, and Magnificent Festivities of King James the First*. 4 vols. 1828. Rpt., New York: Burt Franklin, 1966.

Osgood, Herbert Levi. *The American Colonies in the Seventeenth Century*. 3 vols. New York: Macmillan, 1904–7.

Palfrey, John Gorham. *Compendious History of New England*. 4 vols. Boston: Osgood and Co., 1884.

———. *History of New England during the Stuart Dynasty*. 3 vols. Boston: Osgood and Co., 1858–64.

Bibliography

Percy, George. " 'A Trewe Relacyon': Virginia from 1609 to 1612."
Tyler's Quarterly 3 (1922):259–82.

Purchas, Samuel. *Hakluytus Posthumus; or, Purchas His Pilgrimes.*
4 vols. London: W. Stansby for H. Fetherstone, 1625. Rpt.,
20 vols. Glasgow: J. McLehose, 1905–7.

——. *Purchas His Pilgrimage.* London: W. Stansby for
H. Fetherstone, 1613.

——. *Purchas His Pilgrimage.* 2d ed. London: S. Stansby for
H. Fetherstone, 1614.

——. *Purchas His Pilgrimage.* 3d ed. London: S. Stansby for
H. Fetherstone, 1617.

Quinn, David Beers. "A Colony Is Lost and Found?" In *Set Fair for
Roanoke, Voyages and Colonies, 1584–1606.* By David Beers Quinn.
Chapel Hill: University of North Carolina Press, 1985. 341–78.

——. "The Lost Colony in Myth and Reality, 1586–1625." In
England and the Discovery of America, 1481–1620. By David Beers
Quinn. New York: Knopf, 1974. 432–81.

——, ed. *The Roanoke Voyages, 1584–1590.* 2 vols. Hakluyt Society,
2d ser., nos. 104–5. London, 1955.

——, ed. *The Voyages and Colonising Enterprises of Sir Humphrey
Gilbert.* 2 vols. Hakluyt Society, 2d ser., nos. 83–84.
London, 1940.

Quinn, David Beers, and Alison M. Quinn, eds. *The English New
England Voyages, 1602–1608.* Hakluyt Society, 2d ser., no. 161.
London, 1983.

Quinn, David Beers, Alison M. Quinn, and Susan Hillier, eds. *New
American World.* 5 vols. New York: Arno Press and Hector
Bye, 1979.

Rice, Warner, ed. *Literature as a Mode of Travel.* New York: New
York Public Library, 1963.

Robertson, Wyndham. "The Marriage of Pocahontas: Notes on the
Date of Pocahontas' Marriage, and Some Other Incidents of Her
Life." *Virginia Historical Reporter* 2, no. 1 (1860):67–78. Rpt.,

Southern Literary Messenger 31, no. 2 (or n.s., 10, no. 2) (August 1860):81–91. Rpt., *Historical Magazine* 4 (October 1860):289–96.

——. *Pocahontas, Alias Matoaka, and Her Descendants.* 1887. Rpt., Baltimore: Genealogical Publishing Co., 1968.

Rowe, J. Brooking. *Richard Pecke of Tavistocke.* Exeter, Eng.: J. G. Commin, 1905.

Rowland, Kate Mason. "Captain John Smith, Soldier and Historian." *Conservative Review* 1, no. 1 (February 1899):112–26.

Rule, Henry B. "Henry Adams's Attack on Two Heroes of the Old South." *American Quarterly* 14 (1962):174–84.

Rutman, Darrett B. "The Historian and the Marshal: A Note on the Background of Sir Thomas Dale." *Virginia Magazine of History and Biography* 68 (1960):284–94.

Rymer, Thomas, ed. *Foedera.* 20 vols. London: J. Tonson, 1704–33.

Sabin, Joseph, Wilberforce Eames, and R. W. G. Vail. *Bibliotheca Americana: A Dictionary of Books Relating to America, from Its Discovery to the Present Time.* 29 vols. New York: Sabin and the Bibliographical Society of America, 1868–1936.

Safer, Elaine B. *The Contemporary American Comic Epic: The Novels of Barth, Pynchon, Gaddis, and Kesey.* Detroit: Wayne State University Press, 1989.

Samuels, Ernest. *The Young Henry Adams.* Cambridge: Harvard University Press, 1965.

Schofield, William Henry. *Chivalry in English Literature.* Cambridge: Harvard University Press, 1912.

Seelye, John. *Prophetic Waters: The River in Early American Life and Literature.* New York: Oxford University Press, 1977.

Sharpe, Kevin. *Sir Robert Cotton.* Oxford: Oxford University Press, 1979.

Sheehan, Bernard W. Review of *The Complete Works of Captain John Smith*, ed. Philip L. Barbour. *American Historical Review* 92 (1987):736–37.

Sheridan, Eugene R. "Captain John Smith Goes to Jamestown." *Documentary Editing* 10, no. 2 (June 1988):11–13.

Shirley, John W. "George Percy at Jamestown, 1607–1612." *Virginia Magazine of History and Biography* 57 (1949):227–43.

Shoemaker, Richard H., comp. *A Checklist of American Imprints for 1820–1829*. Metuchen, N.J.: Scarecrow Press, 1964–72.

A Short-Title Catalogue of Books . . . 1475–1640. Ed. A. W. Pollard and G. R. Redgrave. 2d ed., revised by W. A. Jackson, F. S. Ferguson, and Katharine F. Pantzer. 2 vols. London: Bibliographical Society, 1976–86.

Slaughter, Thomas P. "John Smith, Uomo Universale." Review of *The Complete Works of Captain John Smith*, ed. Philip L. Barbour. *Reviews in American History* 15 (1987):220–25.

Smith, Bradford. *Captain John Smith: His Life and Legend*. Philadelphia: Lippincott, 1953.

Smith, Captain John. *An Accidence; or, The Path-way to Experience. Necessary for All Young Sea-men*. London: for Jonas Man, and Benjamin Fisher, 1626.

——. *Advertisements for the Unexperienced Planters of New England, or Any Where*. With the map, allowed by King Charles. London: John Haviland, sold by Robert Milbourne, 1631.

——. *A Description of New England; or, The Observations, and Discoveries, of Captain John Smith*. London: Humfrey Lownes, for Robert Clerke, 1616.

——. *The Generall Historie of Virginia, New-England, and the Summer Isles*. London: printed by J. D[awson] and J. H[aviland], for Michael Sparkes, 1624.

——. *The Generall History of Virginia, the Somer Isles, and New England*. Prospectus. London: [J. Dawson, 1623].

——. *A Map of Virginia*. Oxford: J[oseph] Barnes, 1612.

——. *New Englands Trials*. London: W[illiam] Jones, 1620. New ed., 1622.

——. *The Proceedings of the English Colonie in Virginia since Their First Beginning from England in . . . 1606, till This Present 1612*. Oxford: J[oseph] Barnes, 1612.

——. *A Sea Grammar, with the Plaine Exposition of Smiths Accidence for Young Sea-men, Enlarged*. London: J[ohn] Haviland, 1627.

——. *A True Relation of Such Occurrences and Accidents of Noate as Hath Hapned in Virginia*. London: [E. Allde], for J[ohn] Tappe, sold by W. W[elby], 1608.

——. *The True Travels, Adventvres, and Observations of Captaine Iohn Smith . . . from . . . 1593 to 1629. Together with a Continuation of His Generall History of Virginia*. London: J. H[aviland], for T[homas] Slater, sold [by M. Sparke], 1630.

"Smith's Rescue by Pocahontas." *Southern Literary Messenger* 34 (November–December 1862):626–31.

Smits, David D. "'Abominable Mixture': Toward the Repudiation of Anglo-Indian Intermarriage in Seventeenth-Century Virginia." *Virginia Magazine of History and Biography* 95 (1987):157–92.

Southall, James P. C. "Captain John Smith (1580–1631) and Pocahontas (1595?–1617)." *Tyler's Quarterly* 28 (1946–47):209–25.

Stevenson, Elizabeth, ed. *A Henry Adams Reader*. Garden City, N.Y.: Doubleday, 1958.

Strachey, William. *Historie of Travell into Virginia Britania*. 1612. Ed. Louis B. Wright and Virginia Freund. Hakluyt Society, 2d ser., vol. 103. London, 1953.

Striker, Laura Polanyi. "Captain John Smith's Hungary and Transylvania." In *Captain John Smith: His Life and Legend*. By Bradford Smith. Philadelphia: Lippincott, 1953. 311–42.

——. "The Hungarian Historian, Lewis L. Kropf, on Captain John Smith's *True Travels*: A Reappraisal." *Virginia Magazine of History and Biography* 66 (1958):22–43.

Striker, Laura Polanyi, and Bradford Smith. "The Rehabilitation of Captain John Smith." *Journal of Southern History* 28 (1962):474–81.

Sturtevant, William C., gen. ed. *Handbook of North American Indians*. Vol. 15, *Northeast*. Ed. Bruce G. Trigger. Washington, D.C.: Government Printing Office, 1978.

Swanton, John R. *The Indians of the Southeastern United States*. Bureau of American Ethnology Bulletin no. 137. Washington, D.C., 1946.

Thoreau, Henry David. *The Writings of Henry David Thoreau.* Ed.
F. B. Sanborn and Bradford Torrey. 20 vols. 1906. Rpt., Boston:
Houghton Mifflin, 1949.

Towner, Lawrence W. *"Ars Poetica et Sculptura*: Pocahontas on the
Boston Common." *Journal of Southern History* 28 (1962):482–85.

Tyler, Moses Coit. *A History of American Literature, 1608–1765.* 1878.
Rpt., Ithaca, N.Y.: Cornell University Press, 1949.

Vaughan, Alden T. *American Genesis: Captain John Smith and the
Founding of Virginia.* Boston: Little, Brown, 1975.

——. "Beyond Pocahontas." Review of *The Complete Works of
Captain John Smith*, ed. Philip L. Barbour. *New York Times Book
Review*, June 29, 1986, pp. 27–28.

——. "John Smith Satirized: *The Legend of Captaine Iones.*" *William
and Mary Quarterly*, 3d ser., 45 (1988):712–32.

Virginia Richly Valued. By a Gentleman of Elvas. Trans. Richard
Hakluyt. London: F. Kingston, for M. Lownes, 1609.

Wecter, Dixon. *The Hero in America: A Chronicle of Hero Worship.*
New York: Charles Scribner's Sons, 1941.

Wharton, Henry. *The Life of John Smith, English Soldier.* Ed. and
trans. Laura Polanyi Striker. Chapel Hill: University of North
Carolina Press, 1957.

White, Hayden. *Metahistory: The Historical Imagination in
Nineteenth-Century Europe.* Baltimore: Johns Hopkins University
Press, 1973.

Whitehill, Jane. Review of *Captain John Smith: His Life and Legend*,
by Bradford Smith. *William and Mary Quarterly*, 3d ser., 11
(1954):304–6.

Wing, Donald. *Short Title Catalogue . . . 1641–1700.* 3 vols. 2d ed.
New York: Modern Language Association, 1972–88.

Wood, Anthony à. *Athenae Oxonienses.* Ed. P. Bliss. 4 vols. 1813–20.

Wright, Louis B., ed. *A Voyage to Virginia in 1609: Two Narratives,
Strachey's "True Reportory" and Jourdain's "Discovery of the
Bermudas."* Charlottesville: University Press of Virginia, 1964.

Wroth, Lawrence C. "Bibliographical Note." In *The True Travels.*

By Captain John Smith. New York: Rimington and Hooper, 1930.
73–80.

Young, Philip. "The Mother of Us All: Pocahontas." *Kenyon Review*
24 (1962):391–415. Rpt. in *Three Bags Full*. By Philip Young. New
York: Harcourt Brace Jovanovich, 1967. 175–203.

Index

Anne, Queen (*continued*)
11, 34–40, 54, 69, 70–71, 89, 90,
99, 103
Appamatuck, Queen of, 48, 58, 59, 61
Arber, Edward, 96, 103
Argall, Samuel, xvii, 55, 62, 73, 74,
81, 87
Axtell, James, 12

Bancroft, George, 1, 10, 73, 78
Barbour, Philip L., 11–13, 31, 64, 96
— WORKS: *The Complete Works of
Captain John Smith*, 5, 10, 11; "Poca-
hontas," 11; *Pocahontas and Her
World*, 11; *The Three Worlds*, 10,
11, 91
Barker, J. N.: *The Indian Princess*, 1
Barnes, Charlotte: *The Forest Princess*, 2
Barth, John: *The Sotweed Factor*, 10
Bashaw of Nalbrits, 46
Berblock, Richard, 87
Bertie, Peregrine, 90
Bertie, Peregrine, Jr., 90
Bertie, Robert, 90, 91
Bourchier, Henry, 44, 89, 93
Bourgchier, Henry. *See* Bourchier,
Henry
Bradford, William, 1
Brathwait, Richard, 56
British Museum, 5, 16
Bromfield, Arthur, 87
Brougham, John: *Po-ca-hon-tas*, 2
Brown, Alexander, 14, 17, 50, 95
Bucke, Richard, xvii
Burlesque. *See* Satire

Cabell, James Branch, 65
Callamata, Lady, 46
Canary Islands, 29
Capahowosick, County of, xiv, 24
Capital punishment, xvii, 23, 32–34,
63–64, 103
Captivity. *See* Smith, John: captivity of

Carey, Henry, 90
Carlton, Thomas, 57
Carter, St. Leger, 2
Cassen, George, 21, 22, 33, 41
Caswell, Richard, 87
Causey, Nathaniel, 62, 81
Cavendish, William, 87
Chamberlain, John, 88, 93
Chanoyes, Lady, 46
Charles I, xviii, 37, 38, 39, 44, 89,
99, 104
Chesapeake Bay Indians, 60
Chickahominy, xiv
Civil War, 4, 6
Codrington, John, 62, 80, 81
Committee on Indian Affairs, 63
Cotton, Robert Bruce, 56, 86, 92–93,
94, 100
Council for New England, 39
Covell, Francis, 87
Crashaw, Rawley, 62, 80, 81
Craven, Wesley Frank, 14, 44
Custis, George Washington Parke,
1–2

Dale, Thomas, xvii, 30, 73, 75, 81, 87
Dale's man, 38, 62, 73, 75, 76, 87
Danvers, John, 87
Dare, Virginia, 1
Davies, John, 92
Davis, John, 2
Davis, Richard Beale, 11
Deane, Charles, 2, 14, 48, 95, 102; on
Smith's veracity, 2, 9, 15–16, 46; and
Henry Adams, 14–18, 22, 61, 79, 85,
86; on Smith's *A True Relation*, 15,
16–17, 19, 22, 23; on Smith's men-
tion of Pocahontas episode, 15, 19,
22, 30, 34; on Powhatan's friendly
statements, 22; and Smith's fear
of execution, 24; and Smith's de-
scriptions of geography and Indian
culture, 28; anachronistic fallacy, 30;

Index

Index

Index